I0528775

THERESE NEUMANN

A Stigmatist of Our Day

by

Friedrich Ritter von Lama

Author of
Further Chronicles of Therese Neumann

Translated by
Albert Paul Schimberg

MEDIATRIX PRESS
MMXXIV

ISBN: 978-1-957066-36-3

Nihil Obstat
H. B. Ries
Censor Librorum
Imprimatur
✠ S. G. MESSMER
Archiepiscopus Milwauchiensis
Oct. 31, 1929

Mediatrix Press
607 E 6th Ave
Post Falls, ID 83854
www.mediatrixpress.com

CONTENTS

Chapter V

Chapter VI

In obedience to the decree of Pope Urban VIII and in conformity with the Apostolic Constitution *Officiorum ac munera* of Pope Leo XIII, I declare that I claim no more than a purely human consideration for the extraordinary gifts of grace reported in this book, and that I thereby submit at all times and unreservedly to the judgment of the Catholic Church.

The Author

HE story of a human life is always an interesting thing. When a human life takes on the hue of great sacrificial suffering and thus presents to us the picture of a voluntary victim for the welfare of other souls, it takes on an added interest.

Such is the life of Therese Neumann of Konnersreuth. A simple country girl, born of good sincere Catholic parents, and living her life in the retirement of an obscure village of Catholic Bavaria, she suddenly startles the world by her marvelous and instantaneous cure from a complete blindness of four years' standing, and a painful paralysis and an atrophied limb of six years' standing.

Then there began the extraordinary phenomena of the visions of the Passion of Our Lord, accompanied by profuse tears of blood that gradually formed themselves into streams of blood running down her cheeks; and finally the imprint of the wound marks of the Crucifixion on her hands, her feet, and her side, while the Crown of Thorns was traced in blood upon the head cloth which she wore.

The Vision of the Passion, which she sees and in which she takes a most personal and sympathetic part, consists of a series of ecstasies, during which, while she is apparently dead to all worldly contact, the panorama of the Passion of Our Lord passes before her mental vision in dreadful reality, painfully reflected upon her countenance, in successive periods of from fifteen to twenty minutes. Each period of the vision is followed by a complete relaxation during which she recounts in simplest language what she has seen.

Thus the tragic play goes on from Thursday midnight until Friday afternoon about one o'clock, when she sinks exhausted and almost dead into the pillows of her bed.

It must not be thought, however, that this is the only suffering which she undergoes. She seems to be afflicted with bodily pain and mental and spiritual anguish almost continuously.

If you ask the "WHY" of this condition, her simple answer is "that the world may know that God still lives and that by vicarious suffering and intercessory prayer, she may bring back souls to God."

The Church has made no official pronouncement on this strange phenomenon. Is it all purely supernatural? Is there perhaps an admixture of the natural or the preternatural? Some day the Church may give the answer to these questions.

The so-called scientific world, which always shies at the supernatural, wags its head and trumps out its one favorite answer—"HYSTERIA." Well, if "hysteria" can restore sight to the blind and the perfect use of the limbs to an atrophied body, and can preserve life without nourishment of any kind for over a period of years, then we are justified in asking this "worldly science" to tell us how to become "hysterical."

Friedrich Ritter von Lama has given us a splendid and well-considered history of Therese of Konnersreuth. He presents facts verified by thousands of witnesses. He does not pretend to anticipate the judgment of the Church nor to canonize Therese of Konnersreuth. He presents a life story that will stir the reader to the very depths of his soul, and forces the conviction that religion still dominates the lives of men.

The English translation from the pen of Albert Paul Schimberg is well done and will undoubtedly find a wide circle of readers.

✠JOSEPH SCHREMBS,
Bishop of Cleveland
Cleveland, Ohio,
November 22, 1929,
Feast of St. Cecelia, Virgin and Martyr

TRANSLATOR'S NOTE

"...All possible means are resorted to in an effort to discredit the phenomena of Konnersreuth, to silence the voices which speak of a Divine Hand at work there. Despite all this, the phenomena continue to take place as hitherto, and we have no occasion to change even a line of our book as this new edition appears; much less to retract anything we have said. At most, we might accuse ourselves of an excess of caution, of reserve, here and there. Daily it becomes plainer that at last, among those who kept aloof in doubt, a change is taking place, a gradual turning in the direction in which we felt it our duty to lead the way."

These sentences, it seems to me, deserve the place they have been given at the head of this note, because they embody in a large degree the spirit and the purpose of Friedrich Ritter von Lama's book, *Therese Neumann von Konnersreuth: Eine Stigmatisterte unserer Zeit,* from the third edition of which this translation is made.

I hope that my translation may accomplish among readers of the English-speaking lands something of what Herr von Lama desired his book to accomplish among German readers.

I wish to acknowledge my deep indebtedness to the Right Reverend Joseph Schrembs, D.D., Bishop of Cleveland, for his foreword; and to the Reverend Joseph Reiner, S.J., of Loyola University, Chicago, and the Reverend Stephen Klopfer, of Saint John's Institute for Deaf-Mutes at St. Francis, Wis., for the help they gave me so unstintingly. I have also to thank others for their counsel and encouragement.

ALBERT PAUL SCHIMBERG
Feast of Saint Lawrence,
August 10, 1929

THERESE NEUMANN

A Stigmatist of Our Day

CHAPTER I
INTRODUCTION

OUR years have passed since the first tidings came that Saint Thérèse of the Infant Jesus (generally called the Little Flower, or the Little Saint Thérèse in contrast to the great Saint Teresa of Avila) had manifested her intercessory power on behalf of a sorely afflicted girl, Therese Neumann of Konnersreuth, a village in the pine-clad hills of Bavaria.

Two remarkable cures had taken place, and we were among the many who rejoiced over them. But our rejoicing concerned chiefly the Saint who had once again been the instrument of God's omnipotence. A third healing followed, and a fourth, and we were amazed! Then we directed our attention more and more to the one who had been cured, for we asked, instinctively, why this girl should be, in four successive instances, the object of such extraordinary help from above. Was it not natural to suppose that she was more than an ordinary invalid?

Then the Holy Week of 1926 brought another and even more astounding report: Therese Neumann had received the stigmata, the marks of the Wounds which Our Saviour bore on His body and still bears, and which we as Catholics know full well have been borne by numbers of our brothers and sisters in all periods of the Church's history, down to our own days.

When she received the stigmata, Therese Neumann's prayers and meditations, hitherto purely natural, gave place to ecstatic visions and participation in the Passion of Christ. This association with the Redeemer in His

1

suffering, of which tear-streams of clear blood were the outward sign, was renewed each week on the proper liturgical day, and has continued since the Holy Week of 1926, with but few interruptions; and these, too, are based on the Church calendar. Minor circumstances, the complete abstinence from solid food for several years; ultimately the almost complete abstinence from liquid food as well, and the subsequent maintenance of life solely through Holy Communion, intensified the interest, already keen, of all who had learned of these extraordinary phenomena and made Konnersreuth the goal of many thousands, who, returning home, spread abroad the tidings of all they had seen and experienced.

The press had, from the beginning, given its attention to this singular case; so that, though personally passive, Therese Neumann came to be the storm-center of a vehement controversy, in which professors, physicians, privy councilors, the representatives of several sciences and of many callings, took part. To this was added the uproar of the professedly atheistic and anti-Catholic publications, especially the Socialistic and Communistic organs. These journals raved until it seemed in very truth that the gates of hell had burst open. They raved as though that which they seek to propagate, the spirit of hatred toward God and all that is His, were in deadly peril; and no insult, no slander, no charge was too false or too vulgar to be heaped upon the head of the innocent and defenseless girl. The Catholic viewpoint was scarcely represented in the controversy. A number of theologians expressed their opinions, but theology remained silent. The opinions of the masses, however, are shaped by that section of the press which does not accept the Catholic conception of the universe and which does not consider itself bound by the voice of ecclesiastical authority. All things Catholic are strange to the masses; and the mysticism of the Church is in particular unknown to them and beyond their understanding.

Excepting only a stratum of intellectuals, the Catholic people stood apart from and uninfluenced by the tumult. They believed that the spirit of God had come nearer; they hearkened, they gazed toward Konnersreuth, and their souls, as also those of the *anima naturaliter Christiana,* the many natural Christians who are not formally members of the Church, felt drawn toward the village of Therese Neumann. What they found there agreed completely with their faith; nothing offended them, nothing was different from what their genuinely Catholic hearts deemed proper; and they returned not weakened but rather strengthened in their faith. And more than one whom idle curiosity had brought to Konnersreuth felt impelled to enter the confessional of the village church before beginning the homeward journey.

From the first, the faith of the Catholic people had raised its eyes heavenwards, to God. For it believed that His hand could be seen in these most extraordinary happenings, and that they constituted what are His own and peculiar to Him—*miracles.*

CHAPTER II

CATHOLIC FAITH AND MIRACLES

N these days more than ever before, one finds in intellectual circles many who consider it a privilege of their faith to forego sensuous props of belief, even when God's paternal love deems it well to offer them. They feel themselves so secure in their faith that the ready belief of the people in miracles is in their eyes an offense against faith. They have a favorite quotation from the words of Our Lord: "Blessed are they that have not seen, and have believed." (John 20:19.) From these words they draw justification for accusing their fellow Christians who do not agree with them, of an attitude toward miracles which is unworthy of a Catholic, because it is, they assert, basically due to a weak faith. And from this viewpoint they consider themselves justified in dismissing without investigation, all instances of charismata, such as stigmatization, the bestowal of the marks of Christ's sacred Wounds, and ecstasies; in short, all exceptional gifts of grace.

The attitude of those outside of the Church does not concern us. But that which we have met frequently in lay circles within the Church, and with which we cannot agree, ought to receive, we believe, some attention. For we share the "desire for miracles" which springs from the Catholic people's implicit faith, the simple faith which such an internationally renowned scientist as Louis Pasteur was not ashamed to confess. We hold that the promise made by Our Lord in His hour of departure, that He would be with us until the end of time, must be made manifest constantly through the ages by deeds which are at once worthy of the God of omnipotence and a continuous proof that He abides with us. Miracles are, for us, confirmations of our faith. We realize that our human weakness has need, ever and again, of extraordinary stimulation in the midst of an unbelieving world. We share the believing joy of the people who expect that the God Whom they humbly adore will and must always manifest His omnipotence in a manner which transcends all the powers of man and all the limitations which the natural law, imposed by Him, puts upon the created universe. We do not ascribe to God merely the powers possessed by His human creatures, who are in comparison with Him so feeble and imperfect and are daily in millions of cases helpless and perplexed. With a genuinely supernatural faith, which does not wait until a miracle has been proved, but confides in the combination of active divine Love and active divine Omnipotence, our Catholic people gladly believe in a miracle, even when, in a strictly theological sense, there is none actually present. They do not weigh upon a decimal scale the exact milligram of homage which they must render to God. Their generous faith is eager to give Him all the honor it possibly can. And when a strong probability of a miracle exists, they prefer belief to doubt; they prefer to overcome doubt with faith, rather than to achieve belief at long last by entertaining doubt and slowly, painfully, conquering it. This latter attitude is the one which Our Saviour does not wish us to have, the one He censures; but which has, alas, since the sixteenth century, found a foothold in many circles.

What was Our Lord's own attitude toward miracles? Did He reject or forego them, or did He work wonders in the sight of thousands? Did He not make the greatest miracle of His life, His Resurrection, the very basis of faith in Him and in His teaching, after He had by another miracle deigned to become Man? The Resurrection is the supreme miracle, transcending even the awakening from death of Lazarus, of the daughter of Jairus, and of the young man of Naim, the three of whom the Gospels tell. We can conceive how a living being might control supernatural powers capable of restoring to life a person who has died. But if this is a miracle—and no one would deny that it is—then it is an infinitely greater miracle when the possibility of human action, life, has been radically and completely destroyed by death, and despite this, from out of the state of death which precludes all action, one who is dead, by his own power reunites body and soul and restores himself to life. And this miracle of the Resurrection is the essential confirmation of the faith preached by Christ. Was it not possible, too, that at the Resurrection the senses of the guards at the tomb and of the enemies of Christ were deceived? None the less, the Divine Master did not confine Himself to the spoken word. He considered sensibly perceptible assistance to faith so indispensable that He was not satisfied with the fact that He had risen from the dead but proclaimed it publicly! And to one of His disciples, who wished to content himself solely with the faith and reproached his fellow disciples with having a "desire for miracles," Our Lord gave a crushing answer. Thomas it was, who, after the others had told him of the miracle of the risen Christ, declared: "Except I shall see in His hands the print of the nails, and put my hand into His side, I will not believe." (John xx. 25.) This was the strong faith of the one who charged others with an unseemly desire for miracles! And after eight days Jesus came, the doors being shut, and stood in the midst of them and said, "Peace be to you." Then He said to Thomas: "Put in thy finger hither, and see My hand; and bring hither thy hand, and put it into My side; and be not incredulous but believing." (John 20:27.) Then Thomas fell upon his knees and cried out, "My Lord and my God!" And the Redeemer, referring to the miracle He had worked, spoke these words: "Because thou hast seen, Thomas, thou hast believed; blessed are they that have not seen, and have believed." (John 20:29.)

To be sure, the faith of our Catholic people must not be a defective faith, and it is not! It includes belief in the Saviour's words, "And if he will not hear the Church, let him be to thee as the heathen and publican." (Matt. 18:17.) Therefore it asks, "What does the Church say?" But it does not wait until the Church has spoken, often a lifetime afterwards. For its faith is mature. In our days, in the sight of the reigning Pontiff, it throngs the crypt of Saint Peter's to pray at the tomb of Pope Pius X; to pray no longer *for* him, but to ask his intercession at the throne of God, though the Church has not yet spoken in this matter. And Pius XI? On the vigil of the Feast of Saints Peter and Paul, 1927, he did the same.

But the Catholic people are at all times ready to submit to the voice of the Church; to subject private opinions to the divine authority of the Church in all matters appertaining to it. However, we are not so extremely conservative that we are content to wait until there is no longer any possibility of doubt. We prefer, even before we are shown the proofs of a miracle, to express our living faith in the words of Thomas: "My Lord, and my God!" And in these words is embraced the whole of the faith that fills our souls: confidence in God's almighty power, love for Him insofar as we are capable of it, humble adoration, the deep conviction that except by His will no sparrow falls from the roof; that it is He Who clothes the lilies of the field in such splendor as only He can bestow; and that

He does not wait until human investigators demand of Him evidence of His presence, but reveals Himself whenever it pleases Him to do so, as the Living and Almighty God.

Faith is the first of the theological virtues; and it is above all else, a belief in the attributes of God, in His omnipotence. Faith cannot say, I believe in the miracles of Holy Writ, but in regard to all occurrences of a later date, I refuse, even in concrete instances, to accept them as evidences of God's almighty power until there has been an exact scientific and objective verification. Every miracle was, when it took place, a matter of *hic et nunc*, here and now; and it is possible to deny God's omnipotence in practice, in specific cases, while condescending to a theoretical belief in it.

For the Catholic, profane, human science does not speak the final, but only the secondary word. The last word, the decisive utterance, is that of the Church; and the first word, the initiatory one, is that of the Catholic's own faith operating together with his intellect. Both are gifts of God, and when there is no revelation authenticated by the Church, it is the task of the Catholic to consult the faith-illumined mind, which, according to the teaching of Saint Thomas Aquinas is a feeble image of the Divine Mind. Error is possible, but not always culpable. Unbelief, however, is culpable. And for this reason we refuse to submit our opinions to tribunals which *a priori* deny the whole ideology of the Church of Christ and of divine revelation. A man who tells us that, if asked whether certain events are of a natural or of a supernatural origin, he will from the outset exclude the possibility of the latter, because for him there is no supernatural world in which God is the absolute sovereign, must expect that we will refuse to accept his judgment. He lacks genuinely scientific objectivity. His verdict would be based, not on facts, but upon his prejudgment. His evidence could be of value only insofar as it deals trustworthily with what he himself has seen; not with the meaning thereof. Because he is prejudiced, he is incompetent to pass judgment.

Let us, then, undertake to write of what has happened at Konnersreuth. We shall endeavor, above all, to present the facts as they appear to the senses, as free as possible from any subjectivity. Then we shall consider, so far as may be, the basis and character of the occurrences from the standpoint which the Church takes in these matters. We shall ask ourselves whether there is complete harmony between the spirit of the Church and the spirit of Konnersreuth, even in minute details. But we shall refrain from a final verdict; because, in the first place, such a decision belongs solely to the Church; and, in the second place, because the happenings are not a closed book. They cannot be a closed book so long as the center of them, Therese Neumann, still lives. Her earthly existence is a factor which projects into the future, and only the close of her life will make possible a final verdict.

Cedars of Lebanon have fallen. Therese Neumann is a human being like unto us, with the weaknesses of humanity. She will, until she has drawn her last breath, have the gift of free will, enabling her to decide, even at the last moment, in such a manner as to destroy all that her life until then had built up. Naturally, we do not expect any such thing to happen. Much less do we desire it. We pray for her, that she may have the grace of persevering unto the end.

CHAPTER III

THE INVALID OF KONNERSREUTH

HOW THE SUFFERINGS BEGAN

HERESE NEUMANN was born at Konnersreuth on April 9, 1898. She belongs to a family which deserves special consideration, for she is the eldest of ten children whom God has given her parents. Their house faces the village square of Konnersreuth and it is the smallest and humblest of all the simple homes clustered about it. Strict economy was of necessity the rule in the Neumann household; even the most frugal mode of living was possible only through the cooperation of all of its members, in and out of the house, in the tailoring shop of the father, and on the few acres which he cultivates. It can, therefore, be readily understood that immediately upon leaving school in 1914, Therese should enter the employ of a villager (though his name also was Neumann, he was no relative) to add her earnings to the family's meager income. The war had come, had taken the able-bodied men away, and had left their work to be done by the women. Soon strenuous labor fell to the lot of Therese, in the stable, in the fields, on the threshing floor, and in the tavern of her employer. But strength grows with labor and it was not too much for her to carry sacks of grain weighing 150 pounds up a flight of five steps.[1]

On March 10, 1918, a fire broke out in the neighboring house. Therese joined the villagers who endeavored to extinguish the flames. For two hours she lifted pails of water to those on the endangered roof. Dripping wet, she suddenly collapsed. She had injured her spine seriously. Her condition grew worse and worse. She could scarcely drag herself about; every movement was painful; and seven weeks in the hospital at Waldsassen, a near-by town, brought no improvement. Finally Therese lay in the attic room of her father's cottage, a cripple and totally incapacitated. Cramps caused paroxysms of pain in which she ground her teeth so that they broke. By the middle of March, 1919, her eyesight was completely gone; and her hearing, too, failed at times. Partial paralysis ensued. All that medical science could do was done, but to no avail.

The dream of this young life was shattered. Therese had hoped to enter a Benedictine sisterhood which labors among the heathens of foreign lands. But the Church demands vigorous health of all who would follow this vocation. Therese's religious life had been above the average in this, that already as a child she had cherished a keenly tender appreciation of the sufferings of Christ, so that tears came into her eyes when, at school, there was talk of the Passion. The Way of the Cross was one of her favorite devotions. She took part in the usual Catholic practices, according to the ecclesiastical calendar and the customs of the faithful. Though no longer attending the parish school, she continued to study the catechism. This, then, was the spiritual education she had received. The Church leads all of us along the same path, offers to all of us the same means of grace.

Therese's parents are simple, humble folk, the father plying the trade of a tailor. They are genial, hard-working, sensible, patient people. Their faith is solid, simple, wholesome; and physically and mentally they compare favorably with their townspeople. The veneration of the saints, a matter of course in the Catholic home of the

Neumanns, was intensified and received a new direction when in 1914 the father brought home with him from Waldsassen, two little pictures of Sister Thérèse of the Infant Jesus, at the time not yet beatified. Therese begged one of them from him, and since then it has hung above her bed. She treasured, too, a relic of this Saint, whose veneration in the family was deepened by reading the magazine *Rosenhain.*[2] For a dozen years or more this magazine has sought to spread the spirit of childlike simplicity in the spiritual life. It has known how to avoid the sentimentality which one occasionally meets in devotees of the young Carmelite Saint.

At what time Therese conquered the natural human tendency and desire to be freed from pain, is known to none but God, Who may have helped her to achieve it by withdrawing every prospect of recovery. At all events, the complete resignation to God's will did not come to her without a struggle; it was not given to her as a gift. We shall see presently the measure of genuineness and perfection to which she attained in this regard, within a comparatively brief space of time.

Meanwhile Therese's condition grew worse. At Christmas time in 1922 her throat began to swell and there followed paralysis of the swallowing muscles, so that thereafter it became impossible for Therese to take solid food. In the next two years ulcers developed in her throat, producing almost fatal choking spells. Therese could take scarcely any liquid food. In 1923 the amount was no more than two or three tablespoonfuls each day. Her steadily increasing weakness indicated that death was inevitable and close at hand. During the fortnight before the Holy Saturday of 1925, Therese could not swallow even a single drop of water; and since August 6, 1926, the Feast of the Transfiguration, six or eight drops of water daily are all that pass her lips. This water she swallows after she has received Holy Communion which must be given to her in small particles of the Sacred Host. One may, therefore, say that her life is sustained solely through the Holy Eucharist.

Naturally, at first, at the request of the distracted mother and of the parish priest, the sufferer was induced to attempt to take nourishment. But this caused immediate vomiting and choking spells. Today the need for food and drink has disappeared entirely. And the need for sleep, too, has almost disappeared. Therese sleeps only during the nights between Fridays and Saturdays. Until the Easter of 1927, there was a continuous decrease in the weight of her body. The remarkable aspect of this matter is, that until then she still took liquid nourishment. After she ceased to take even liquid food, her weight remained at 110 pounds, excepting during the ecstasy of the Passion.

The suffering which this blind, paralyzed, partially deaf girl could offer to God when He came to her in Holy Communion was great, indeed. But it was not yet enough. More sufferings were to follow. Contraction of the muscles crippled her left leg and drew it up under the right one. Constant pressure of the body caused the flesh of her left foot to wear away, down to the bones. Her back was tortured by many festering bedsores.

Such was the pitiable spectacle presented by Therese Neumann of Konnersreuth after five years of suffering.

THE FIRST CURE

On April 29, 1923, Saint Peter's Church at Rome was festively decorated for the beatification of Sister Thérèse of the Infant Jesus, of the Carmelites at Lisieux. This was an exceptional occasion, for Sister Thérèse had died not more than twenty-five years before. What took place that day in the cottage of Tailor Neumann in Konnersreuth we shall let Therese herself tell us, in part:

"It was on April 29, 1923, at six o'clock in the morning. Father was going to make a little journey on my account and came to my bedside. 'Resl,[3] I am going now,' he said. I was awake, but I did not even see him. He went toward Mitterteich, to the railway station.

"After that, half an hour may have gone by. Suddenly I opened my eyes. I saw my hands and my white nightgown. 'Am I dreaming?' I rubbed my eyes and looked around. I saw once more the sacred pictures on the walls and greeted them as dear old friends after a long separation.

"Then a woman came into the room. I did not know who she was. 'Who are you?' I asked, and her answer betrayed her astonishment. Then I knew by her voice that it was my sister Zenzl.[4] During the time I had been blind, more than four years, she had grown very much. That is why I did not know her."

Frau Neumann was called and Therese cried out to her: "Mother, I can see!" The mother was dumbfounded and did not believe her daughter's sight had been restored. "Resl, you are dreaming!" With hands that trembled she held a potted plant before Therese's eyes, and at once the girl stretched out a hand toward the flowers. Then another sister, Otillie, was called, and there was consternation anew. "Why, Ottl, how tall you have grown!" All of them wept for joy. The father returned home in the evening. On the following day her physician, Sanitätsrat Dr. Seidl[5] of Waldsassen, called. Wondering amazement again, and the question: How did it happen? The mother spoke her mind: "Yesterday Thérèse of the Infant Jesus was beatified; and she, we believe, helped our Therese."

Faith, which the Church approves, may give this explanation, even though there is for the present no compelling reason for accepting a causal connection between the two occurrences. (Therese, in semi-ecstatic condition when she told me on August 26, 1927, of her conversation with Saint Thérèse, maintained that such a connection existed. *Author.*)

The blindness of Therese Neumann had lasted four years and one month.

THE SECOND CURE

It was May 3, 1925. The constantly festering wound of the left foot caused the worried mother to fear that an amputation would become necessary. For the sake of her mother, who did not conceal her troubled thought, Therese prayed for a slight improvement at least; and with confidence in the intercessory power of Sister Thérèse, she permitted three rose leaves, which had been blessed and had been touched to the tomb of the Little Flower, to be placed on the bandage when the wound was dressed. Had not the rose been the favorite flower of the Carmelite of

Lisieux? After a few minutes, the wound ceased to hurt, and when the dressing was removed it was seen to be closed and covered with a thin, fresh membrane. After a short time, the healing was complete. The rose leaves had been sent to Therese by a Carmelite priest.

The acceptance of a causal connection possesses, in this instance, a greater degree of justification. Of course, the curative power was not in the rose leaves, but in the faith with which they were applied. "Go thy way; for thy faith hath made thee whole!" (Luke 17:19.) And it does not matter to us whether the healing process was a natural or a supernatural one. God avails Himself of the one no less than of the other, for He is the Lord.

THE THIRD CURE

On May 17, 1925, Saint Peter's at Rome was again the scene of a solemn ceremony. Again the object of the festive pomp and joy was Sister Thérèse of the Infant Jesus, who was at this time proclaimed Saint by Pope Pius XI. His Holiness declared that the name of the Carmelite *beata* was now inscribed on the Church's official list of canonized saints, and at the Mass which followed he, for the first time, sought her intercession in the use of the prescribed liturgical prayers.

Therese Neumann's paralyzed condition had not changed. The spine was still as though broken, powerless, so that it could not support the upper body; and sitting was impossible. The left foot was still drawn up through muscular contraction. The left arm had, meanwhile, become paralyzed. In addition to all this, Therese had for approximately a year and a half been suffering from ulcers in the head from which the pus issued through the eyes and ears. From October, 1918, to this day, May 17, 1921, she had not left her bed of pain. As witnesses of this we have her parents and brothers and sisters, Dr. Seidl, the Reverend Father Naber, parish priest of Konnersreuth, and the entire population of the village.

Therese had begun a novena in honor of the new Saint, but without a thought of asking for the restoration of her health. Her disposition was purified to this extent; her surrender to the Will of God had reached this degree of perfection.

May 17, 1925, was a Sunday and there were May devotions in the village church at two o'clock in the afternoon. We shall listen to Father Naber's account of what came to pass. He prefaces his report with this statement: "Not until today did she say to me, 'During the last three years I am sure I have not prayed even one Our Father to get well again.' "

"Contrary to their custom, Therese's parents had remained at home during the afternoon devotions on this Sunday," says Father Naber. "During the service in honor of the Queen of May, Therese in her bed prayed the glorious mysteries of the Rosary. She had begun to meditate on the second mystery when, suddenly, there was a bright Light about her, as she told us immediately afterwards. An electric light, and even the light of the sun, was dim in comparison to this Light. She was frightened at first and cried out. This brought her parents to her bedside. Later (which she could not afterwards recall) she called out, 'Mother, where is Father Naber?' They called me then, and a Mallersdorfer Sister came, too. I saw Therese looking steadily at an object toward which her arms were outstretched. Her face beamed with joy, she nodded her head, bowed with exquisite courtesy and moved her hands as would a lady-in-waiting who conversed with her gracious princess. Involuntarily I said to the nursing Sister, 'Thus God honors His Saints!' All at once Therese sat up, which she had not been able to do for six and one-half years. She had, before my arrival, sat up, but it had caused her excruciating pain.

"After she was again lying down, her face retained the transfigured look," continues Father Naber. "This vanished and she began to weep bitterly because the glorious Light was gone and all was drab once more. She grasped for the stick, always at hand, which she used to summon her people. She was, therefore, unaware that we were present. Then I spoke to her: 'Resl, what has happened?' Instead of answering my question she declared with an assurance so absolute that it amazed us: 'I can now sit up!' and did so. 'I can walk, too!' she announced, and then Frau Neumann examined her daughter's feet. The leg which had been drawn up was now in normal position. After a gown had been thrown about her, she began to walk, as yet, out of carefulness, with assistance. Her steps were the first in six and one-half years. I asked again, 'Resl, where have you really been?' And this time she told me (after the others had at her request left the room) with astonishing assurance what had taken place.

"After the wonderful Light had appeared, a mild, friendly Voice began to speak. She had seen no one. 'Resl, do you wish to get well?' 'I answered,' said Therese, 'it is all the same to me—to get well, to remain sick, or to die. Whatever the good God wills.' The Voice: 'Resl, wouldn't it give you joy if your sufferings were lessened; if you could at least sit up and walk?' I answered, 'Everything gives me joy that comes from the good God.' The Voice: 'Resl, I shall cause you to have a little joy. You shall be able to sit up and walk!' When I thereupon sat up, it seemed to me that something took me by the hand and helped me. The Voice: 'But you shall still have much to suffer. However, fear not. I have hitherto helped you and I shall help you in the future.' There is scarcely anything as painful to Therese as praise. She is fearful lest praise bestowed upon her be denied Our Lord and Saint Thérèse. ... The Voice spoke particularly of the value of resignation, humility, and suffering. After it had spoken this sentence twice, 'It is through suffering that so many souls are saved,' it concluded, as though wishing to permit itself to be identified: 'I have already written that far more by suffering and by persecution than by eloquent discourses does Jesus wish to build up His Kingdom.' Therese could not remember where these words were to be found, and was delighted when I showed them to her. They are in the Little Flower's sixth letter to missionaries."

To help toward a correct estimate of this cure, we shall add material from other sources.

The Light out of which the Voice spoke was in Therese's line of vision, above the bed, and it was white. When her father, first to come at her call, burst into the room, he called to her in complete ignorance of what was taking place, and offered her a glass of water. But she paid no attention. To her answer, "Everything gives me joy that comes from the good God," she had, she relates, added these words: "All the flowers give me joy, and the birds, or again, a new suffering, for that makes for variety. But my greatest joy is in the dear Saviour." Now the Voice insisted: "You may experience a bit of joy. You may sit up. Try it. I shall help you." At these words Therese felt herself grasped by the hand, and her mother declares that she raised herself a little. At the first attempt to sit up, there was still extreme pain in the back. The next words were, as Father Naber, in supplementing his report, declares, "But you shall be permitted to suffer much and for a long time, and no physician shall be able to help you. But do not be afraid. I have helped you hitherto and I shall continue to do so. Only through suffering can you perfect your character and realize your vocation of sacrifice, and thereby assist the priests. More souls are saved through suffering than through the most brilliant sermons. I have already written this."[6]

Worldlings cannot understand such words as these. Their attitude toward pain is a merely natural one, and all their efforts are directed toward release from suffering. And if this is denied them, they accuse God of injustice. As an explanation, let there be recorded what Saint Francis of Assisi said to Brother Leo, when the latter asked him, "Wherein is perfect joy?"

"Above all the graces and gifts of the Holy Spirit, which Christ has given to his friends, is that of conquering oneself, and suffering willingly for the sake of Christ all pain, ill-usage and opprobrium, and calamity; because of all the other gifts of God we can glory in none, seeing they are not ours, but God's; as said the Apostle: 'What hast thou that thou hast not received of God? And if thou hast it of God, why dost thou glory, as if thou hadst it of thyself?' But in the cross of tribulation and affliction we may glory, for these are ours; and therefore, says the Apostle, 'I will not glory save in the cross of Our Lord Jesus Christ.' "[7]

But let us return to Therese's little room. There stood about the bed, as witnesses of these mysterious occurrences, Father Naber, the parents, the Mallersdorfer Sister and the aspirant who accompanied her, and Therese's married sister, Anna. All were moved to tears. Wholly unconscious of their presence, Therese was about to take hold of the stick, to summon her mother. Then the parish priest announced, "Resl, we are here!" She realized now that she was not alone. When she saw their tears, she asked, "What is the matter with all of you?" and added, "I shall walk now!" It had been taken for granted that she would never again use her outer clothes, so they had been given away during the war. A dress was brought hastily from downstairs and put on her. She stood on her feet, unsupported, upright, at her bed, and walked with assistance about the room. The two dislocated vertebrae had resumed their normal positions. All evidences of paralysis and of cramps had disappeared, nor did they reappear. From this time on, Therese could walk with assistance.

The Mallersdorfer Sister declares that when she took Therese's pulse during the mysterious conversation, it was regular, as was also her breathing. There was not the slightest sign of fear or excitement. One saw her lips move, but could hear no words. Joy and earnestness were alternately mirrored in her countenance. The parents saw their daughter speak and listen joyfully, but they heard only two words, Yes and No, distinctly. When the Light vanished, Therese wept bitterly, as has been stated, because in comparison to it, all was dull now and almost dark.

For six and one-half years, without a day's interruption, Therese had been bound to her bed, helpless, almost motionless. Now she could raise herself up. The left foot was normal again, and even the festering bedsores of her back, which had the day before stained the fresh chemise with blood, were closed and healed. Using a cane because of her bodily weakness, she was able to walk about, but as her parents insisted that she spare herself, it was not until June 11 that she went out of doors. Then, leaning on her father's arm, she walked across the village square to the church, to thank God.

WAS IT A MIRACLE?

It has been asked, Was this cure a miracle? And it has been maintained that the answer must be a negative one. And why? Because, forsooth, there was no "factual verification" of the displacement of the joints of the lower spine! But is one justified in asserting that the injury did not exist when five physicians in succession have testified to its effects during six and one-half years? How easy it would be, according to this sort of reasoning, to rid the world of all infirmities! One need but neglect to have them "factually verified"! And because in this case there was no scientific "factual verification" (no X-ray picture had been taken) a purely supernatural explanation is declared unnecessary. To deny thus offhand the fact, to the effects of which five doctors of medicine give testimony, and to regard it as nonexistent, is contrary to all sense. But this is done and a solitary circumstance is singled out as the determining factor to disprove the supernatural nature of the cure. None of the accompanying facts and events, not even the healing of the festering bedsores, is permitted to count, to bear any weight. Where, then, is there any sincerity? One makes use of the deprecatory word, "autosuggestion"; that is, conscious or unconscious self-deception. What is suggestion? It is the transfer of wills, the imposition of a stronger will upon a weaker one. And autosuggestion? It consists in this, that a person, with the aid of his own will, impresses the product of his own phantasy so powerfully upon his mind that he mistakes the imagined thing for fact and reality and makes it the basis of further action or effect. Invalids of abnormal imagination are common. Every physician of some experience will be able to distinguish in these matters. In the case of Therese Neumann, it did not occur to any of the five physicians that hallucination could explain the spinal injury, the paralysis, the cramps, the festering sores. If self-deception lay at the root of her maladies and at the root of her cures, the tests which followed must have proved this. First she had the consciousness of cure transmitted to her through the Voice. She answered: "I can now walk!" Was this deception?

No, for the ensuing test proved that she actually could walk; the wounds that had been open were healed now, the paralysis existed no longer, the spine once more supported the body.

Autosuggestion? It is an activity of the will in relation to self. But as we know, Therese had long since surrendered her own will to that of God. This is an essential of progress in the spiritual life. Perfection is impossible without humility and obedience. Was the surrender of her own will complete and enduring? This, too, was subjected to a test. When the Voice (which she had cause to believe possessed the power to cure her) asked her what she desired, in that decisive moment, when in the midst of her pain and after six and one-half years of suffering, the prospect of release was presented, her answer proved complete, unconditional abandonment to the will of God. Not even in this moment, when the temptation was keenest, did her own will assert itself. It remained submissive to the Divine Will. "It is all the same to me—to get well, to remain sick, or to die. Whatever the dear God wills." There was, then, an entire absence of the primary requisite of autosuggestion; will, self-will, was not operative. But when the will is not operative, there can be no transfer of it, neither in relation to another nor to oneself.

And were the Light and the Voice products of Therese's imagination? Her behavior contradicts such an assumption. She cried out in fear, so loudly that she was heard downstairs. Did she become frightened at something which came from her own consciousness; something which was, accordingly, already there and familiar to her? One does not cry out in fear at the product of one's own phantasy. One does so, at most, when something dreaded becomes an actuality a fact. And even then the cry is not an expression of surprise, for the mind has prepared itself, has made itself familiar with it, and knows what is to come.

So the Light and the Voice, the consciousness of cure because assurance of a cure had been given, and the actual cure as an immediate fact within the limits of the announcement—all these belong together. Whosoever wishes to answer the question, Was it a miracle?, must not sever this connection and put in its place other arbitrarily presumed combinations. False premises lead to false conclusions.

❦

THE FOURTH CURE

On September 30, 1897, Sister Thérèse of the Infant Jesus passed from this earth, and her desire for eternal contemplation of God and never-ending union with Him was fulfilled. It was a day of supreme joy, the climax of happiness in the life of little Thérèse, and of gratitude to God for His bestowal of so many graces upon a human being by nature unworthy. If ever, then surely on the anniversaries of her death, the Little Flower must feel impelled to shower roses down upon the living, barred as yet from the ineffable bliss she now enjoys.

"It was September 30, 1925, at 12:30 o'clock in the morning," says Therese. "I was still awake and was reading the Litany in honor of Saint Thérèse by the light of an electric lamp. Nothing could have been more unexpected than what happened. There was, all of a sudden, a Light in front of me, the same Light as there was when I was cured of the paralysis. It came very suddenly, as it had the first time, as suddenly as lightning. In comparison with it, electric light is darkness. ... I saw and gazed: Light, but no form, no figure. ...Then I heard a Voice, the same Voice. ... It said: 'You can walk now without assistance. The pain that comes from your eyes shall be lessened. But in place of it there shall come intense suffering. ... Encourage the people to have confidence in God! ...' 'But,' I interposed, 'I do not myself know whether I am on the right track, or whether I am doing everything in a wrong manner.

Some say my case is a fraud; others are angry with me. It is enough to make me doubt whether I am doing everything as it ought to be done.' ... Thereupon the Voice: 'Follow your confessor's counsel in blind obedience and confide all to him. You must free yourself more and more from self. Preserve your childlike simplicity.' ... The Voice ceased and the Light disappeared."

Therese rubbed her eyes, gazed about, stood up, essayed to walk, and then strode up and down the room, without support of any kind, for a quarter of an hour. After the first ringing of the church bell early in the morning she walked alone down the stairs from her attic room, across the square to the church, the first time in seven years without assistance. Her second visit was to the home of the parish priest, and then, laden with the choicest roses from

Father Naber's garden, she returned to the church to decorate the picture of the Holy Family.

Therese had been so grateful, so content at being able to walk with the aid of another person or by using a cane, that any desire for further favors was out of the question. Such a desire could not arise within her, because the subjection of her will to the Divine Will had long since become absolute. Her own doubt shows that she was not "living in the imagination." And again, the healing followed upon the announcement that it would take place. The Voice admonished her wholly in the spirit of the Church, which, when it tests supernatural gifts, considers obedience to the ecclesiastical authority derived from Christ as the surest proof of genuine virtue. "Follow your confessor's counsel in blind obedience." Those who are shackled by their egos put themselves first, and say, "I will follow my own inclinations, my own knowledge, my own will." But through the mouth of the Church, God speaks: "Follow Me! Give obedience to him who, authorized by My Church, stands in My stead." Whatsoever leads to humility is from God, and obedience is naught but humility in action. By their fruits the Church distinguishes between truth and self-deception.

THE FIFTH CURE

Therese had been told that intense suffering was to come. It did not fail, nor long delay.

The unmistakable connection of the first four cures with the Saint of Lisieux might lead to the suspicion that Therese Neumann's special devotion to the Little Flower had caused her on these occasions to contribute to the cures through a special psychical and, in combination with that, a special physiological disposition; for somehow the invalid's thoughts must have dwelt upon Saint Thérèse on the days which memorialized the Saint's death, beatification, and canonization. But there came a day which stood apart from any relation to this Saint. Father Naber, an eyewitness, shall tell us about it.

"On November 7, 1925, Therese was compelled to return to her bed. Excruciating pain, which she endured for three days, left her so weak that she could not even open her eyes. Finally, in the evening of November 13, Dr. Seidl, who came in answer to a summons, declared after a thorough examination that it was a case of appendicitis and that Therese must be taken to the hospital at Waldsassen at once, to be operated on. He would not, he said, assume responsibility for the result if the operation were delayed until the next morning. Dr. Seidl is an authority on appendicitis. The parents were dumbfounded and called for me, in the hope that I might advise against taking Therese to the hospital. After consulting with Dr. Seidl, I told the parents they ought to consider the physician's verdict as the voice of God and have their daughter taken to the hospital at once. The father ran to arrange for transportation and the mother gathered bedding and clothes, but the invalid called me to her bedside and asked whether she might not beg little Saint Thérèse to help her, so that she would not have to be operated on, if such were the will of God. Not, she declared, that she objected to the operation, but because her mother was lamenting so inconsolably. When I answered, Yes, she had a relic of Saint Thérèse placed on the painful spot, and while those present prayed to the Little Flower, the invalid in her bed turned like a worm in agony. She herself says she prayed mentally, no more than this: 'It is all the same to me, Saint Thérèse. You can help me. It is all the same to me, but you hear how mother carries on.' All of a sudden Therese sat up somewhat and opened her eyes. Her face became as transfigured. She lifted up her hands and stretched them out toward an invisible object, and was heard to say a few times, 'Yes.' Then she sat up completely, pressed her fingers against the abdomen repeatedly, and said: 'Really!' I asked her whether Saint Thérèse had, perhaps, come again, and helped her. The answer was, 'Yes, and she told me I must go to church at once and thank God. Mother, bring me a dress.' "

In reply to her father's question, Therese stated: "A hand appeared and I wished to grasp it but I could not. It was a white and delicate hand, like those Saint Thérèse has in her pictures. The first three fingers were outstretched, the others closed."

The Reverend Father Naber reports further: "All pain and all fever had disappeared. The same Light and the same Voice had come again, and the Voice had said: 'Your complete submission and joyous endurance of pain pleases us. That the world may know that there is a Higher Power, you shall not have to be operated on. Arise and go to the church, but at once, at once, and thank the Lord. You shall still suffer very much, but you must not be afraid, not even when the interior suffering comes. It is only in this way that you can cooperate in the saving of souls. But you must die more and more to self. Preserve your childlike simplicity.' "

Therese's mother objected to her going to the church. "Now, at night"—it was then seven o'clock —"out of the heat here, with your fever!" Father Naber decided: "If Saint Thérèse was here to help you, let us go at once, as we are!" And so a little procession of ten persons, all of whom are still alive and available as witnesses, wended its way, with Therese in the center, across the village square and entered the church. Meanwhile, the news had spread and the villagers flocked to the Neumann cottage. Each one wished to hear tell of this miracle. It was late before quiet could be restored. During the night the pus passed from the inflamed appendix in the natural way.

Early the next morning Therese received Holy Communion. Then there was a journey to Waldsassen to report to the physician and to have the cure recorded.

This time there was a "factual verification" of the disease: acute appendicitis, the disease in an aggravated form. Only an immediate operation could be of help. The cure took place in the natural sequence: the inflammation subsided, the wounded place healed, the pus was eliminated, the fever disappeared, bodily strength was restored. But the process, which normally requires several weeks, was telescoped into a few seconds. The aftermath of a natural cure is as long as after an operation and demands special care on the part of the convalescent for months afterwards. Once again, the test corroborated what the Voice had promised. Once again, experience followed on the heels of the announcement. Once again there was the fact of a complete and instantaneous cure.

CHAPTER IV

THE STIGMATIST OF KONNERSREUTH

THERESE RECEIVES THE STIGMATA

I N a letter of November 19, 1924, her only letter that has thus far appeared in print, Therese Neumann writes: "... You must know that I have been sick for seven years and must always lie in bed. ... I must always lie down. The least movement causes severe pain and cramps. Not a single day am I free from pain. ... I like very much to read now. You see, I have plenty of time, but often my head hurts me very much, so that I cannot think, not to speak of reading. Well, as God wills."[8]

On another occasion she said that, since her suffering began, she had really never been free from pain. And if we look back over the course of events in her case, we can distinguish plainly the process by which her spirit was set free, more and more, from all things of earth, a mark of the soul in its ascent toward God. It is the first of the three stages which mystical theology describes for us. It is purgation. To this must succeed illumination, and as the harmonious conclusion, union with God, if the ascent continues and there is perseverance.

Therese had long since passed the point at which the spirit, no longer mastered by the suffering body, and the soul, no longer subject to the weight of physical pain, rises step by step onward and upward. First of all, the compulsory suffering had to convert itself into readiness to suffer, which springs from the acknowledgment of mankind's eternal guilt in the sight of God. This leads to love of God, to love of Christ the Redeemer, and to the will-to-suffer. Then suffering becomes naught else, naught less than love in action. The redemptive act of Christ is not merely an historical event which the world's chronology has placed in the year 33. But as it was enacted for all men of all times, it has to a certain extent the quality of an uninterrupted present, for it has the same relationship to each newborn babe as it had to the contemporaries of Jesus. Love ought to be directed to the suffering Saviour Who, through the Holy Sacrifice of the Mass, keeps forever living and daily renews the memory of His Passion. And the higher man's reciprocal love for Him mounts, the higher also must rise the will-to-suffer. This relationship brings about what men experience as happiness-in-pain.

Lest it be supposed that we are building a theory out of the life of a single person, we shall relate the experience of Father Utsch, S.J., when visiting a leper asylum at Biwasaki, Japan. He had come to the bedside of a man who had found the True Faith as a result of the frightful suffering which the fatal disease brought upon him. His face was gruesomely eaten away, his body almost a single large wound. The Sister told the blind leper that a priest was beside his bed. The dying man whispered then, with labored breathing and the shadow of a voice: "Ah, Father, I am so happy! I am so happy! Soon I shall go to Heaven, soon I shall be permitted to see Jesus and the Mother of God! I thank God! I thank Him!" When the Jesuit congratulated him and asked his prayers for himself and for the Christian congregation at Shimonoseki, he breathed a "Yes," and "I pray for the whole Church."[9]

That which elevates this Christian will-to-suffer infinitely above the voluntary but horrible penances of, as an example, the Indian fakirs, is that which the latter lack completely: love of God. Christian suffering is not a perpetual inescapable penance. It is true, penance is doubtless necessary as the first step, but with an upright will in combination with genuine contrition and the limitless mercy of God and His love, the penitential period is soon ended. The will-to-suffer leads, then, automatically to the privilege of suffering in the sense of participating in the love-inspired suffering of the Saviour and to the privilege of sharing in the atonement for the transgressions of others, transgressions which grieve the Redeemer. This vicarious suffering is part of the treasury of the Catholic Church. With the Fall of Adam, through which sin came into the world, the obligation of his descendants to take part in this atonement began. The consciousness of a common debt toward God and of the obligation to atone, was preserved by the heathen peoples; and not only the idea of sacrifice was maintained but the realization that innocence made a victim especially pleasing to God, and was therefore, the most efficacious in propitiating Him. Against the erring excesses of heathenism, God Himself established among His chosen people the only sacrifice of atonement which pleased Him. This spirit of atoning sacrifice reached its apogee in the Incarnation of Jesus Christ and the Passion and death He endured for all men. But as sin was not thereby exterminated but continues to exist, it must continue to be atoned for by the humanity which commits it. The atonement is achieved, through Christ's mediation, by the perpetual renewal, in the Holy Mass, of the Sacrifice of Atonement on Golgatha; insofar as men have a part in it, through suffering, including vicarious suffering, God distributes suffering according to the ability of each man's shoulders to carry it. Much more meritorious than this passive suffering is the active will-to-suffer in order to share voluntarily in the pain of the Saviour's Passion, and also in order to practice in this way the imitation of Christ. But the will-to-suffer must go only as far as the will of God teaches: "Father, Thy will be done on earth as it is in Heaven! ... But not My will be done but Thy will!" And the Will of God is voiced by the authorized priest, the confessor. It guards against the excesses of heathen practices, of penitential systems which are not guided by love, not filled with love; it watches zealously, lest the spiritual stream overflows its lawful banks before it reaches the goal.

Jesus Christ, Who is with His Church to the end of the world, deigns at times to bestow the outward signs of the deeper inner character of this suffering; and these signs or marks are the same as those which were the exterior evidences of His own suffering for love of us. They are the Sacred Wounds, the stigmata. The history of stigmatization shows that the bestowal of the marks of the Wounds is the act of a sovereign, free will; that there is no process, no mechanical, automatic sequence following essential prerequisites, but a free giving. It is a matter, as the Church teaches, of an actual *gratia gratis data;* of a grace freely bestowed by God, as Pope Benedict XIV declared. Of a rule we can speak only insofar as the spiritual conditions to which we have referred, must be present. However, even when they exist, there is not the least warrant for expecting that the stigmata will be received.

After this introduction, which seems necessary, let us return to the consideration of Therese Neumann's case.

🌸🌿🌸

According to the opinion of Father Naber, who has known Therese for eighteen years, she was in no wise distinguished from the other children in the parish school, not even in the expression of her piety. If she was distinguished from them at all, it was by her diligence. Her spiritual training was conducted within the framework of the Church Year and according to the precepts of the Church. Every parish priest, every spiritual adviser, endeavors to prevent excesses, which are followed, generally, by extremes in the opposite direction. The extraordinary in the religious life must not be sought, must not be desired; for it is a basic law that in these matters the will of God must be supreme, must decide all things. Self-will is the beginning of a spiritual descent. Therese's will did not desire the stigmata, for when they had come, she did not know what they were, did not comprehend their significance. "I do not need these. Saint Thérèse of the Infant Jesus did not have them!"

With the coming of Lent in 1926, a severe pain in the head returned. It was caused by an ulcer of the ears and had troubled her three years before. On the day on which the Church closes the season of Passiontide, that is, Holy Saturday, the ulcer opened and the pus flowed out of the ears. Therese says of this period of pain: "During the whole of Lent I could scarcely pray at all, not even the Way of the Cross. All I could do was to make the intention: Our Saviour suffered even more than this for us."

It was during the Lent of 1926, at night, and Therese lay quietly in her bed, without giving a thought to anything in particular. She could not, because of her suffering. "All at once," she says, "I saw the Redeemer before me. I saw Him in the Garden of Mount Olive. When this happened to me the first time, I did not know that it had a special meaning. But I saw the Saviour, as He knelt there. I saw all the other things, too, very distinctly: the trees, the rocks, everything as in a garden. And I saw the three Apostles, but they were not lying down or sleeping, as they are usually pictured, but sat rather, leaning on stones, and were entirely powerless. ... Suddenly I felt, while I saw the Saviour, such a pain in my side that I thought, now I am going to die. At the same time I felt something hot run down my side. It was blood. It kept on trickling until towards noon of the next day. From Friday noon onward, the whole next week was quiet." Without being conscious of the day on which this transpired, Therese saw the second mystery of the sorrowful Rosary, the Scourging of Our Lord, on the following Thursday night; on the third Thursday night, the third mystery, the Crowning with Thorns; on the fourth Thursday, the fourth mystery, the carrying of the Cross; but on the fifth Thursday night, not the fifth mystery, the Crucifixion, but once again the first mystery, the Agony in the Garden.

With the help of her sister Crescentia, familiarly called Zenzl, Therese succeeded in concealing the heart-wound and its bleeding until Holy Thursday. On Good Friday, while Therese was in a state of complete ecstasy, therefore unconscious of herself and of the created universe, the blood flowed so copiously from her side and also from her eyes that her parents began to have an intimation of what manner of suffering their daughter was enduring. But as yet they knew nothing of the wounds of the hands and of the feet, which had, meanwhile, appeared.

"I do not know exactly when I got them" is Therese's naïve avowal. "On Good Friday night they were simply there. ... During the vision I did not have the least intimation of them, for I was not thinking at all of myself. How could I? I could do nothing but look at the Saviour. When I ... came to again, I felt that blood was running down my hands and feet, too. I could not see what is was, however, because of the blood which closed my eyes. Not until at night did I say to my sister, 'Zenzl, see what is the matter with my hands and feet, they hurt me so much.' "

Therese's parents called Father Naber. He said to her: "In obedience, let me see the wounds of your hands and feet!" What he saw moved him so vehemently that it required considerable time for him to regain his composure. He has written of this matter: "When another priest and I visited her on Good Friday after the midday meal, she lay there like a martyr, her eyes closed by blood, two streams of blood on her cheeks. She was as pale as a dying person. Until three o'clock, the hour at which the Saviour died, she endured the most excruciating death agonies. Then she was quieter again. ... During the death agonies of that Good Friday she saw the Passion of Christ from the Garden of Olives to Calvary enacted before her. She participated in His suffering and shared His utter abandonment on the Cross. She felt at the time, intense pain on the back of her hands and the insteps of her feet. Now both hands bear, on the upper surfaces, and both feet on the insteps, round, open wounds from which clear blood flows. ... The physician has examined all of them very carefully."

Since then Therese Neumann has borne the stigmata. They cause her constant pain, but she has become accustomed to this comparatively mild form of suffering. The feeling is, she says, "as though something were sticking in them." The seat of pain in the side-wound is deeply inward. This wound is not where Christ was pierced by the lance, on the right side, but is directly over her heart. It seems to Therese that the wound penetrates through her heart, but this has been true only since the Feast of the Sacred Heart of 1927. For fourteen days, until April 17, the wounds were fresh and open. Then a tender membrane formed over them, which, however, disappeared each Friday. The wounds bled only on the Fridays of Lent. From Easter to Pentecost, 1927, that is, during the Church's joyous season, there were no Friday visions of the Passion.

Her parents and her physician attempted to heal Therese's wounds by applying ointments. The result was such extreme pain that she lost consciousness and not until the remedy (a salve) was removed did the pain cease gradually. In this extremity Therese took refuge to the one who had repeatedly helped her, Saint Thérèse of Lisieux. She did not ask for a healing, but only for a word as to how the wounds were to be treated. Soon after her prayer of April 17, 1926, the wounds dried, without, however, healing or becoming scarred or incrusted. Dr. Seidl declares: "This is extraordinary, the wounds do not fester, they do not become inflamed. Some people declare it is a fraud, and others say it is a matter of hallucination. Neither of them speak the truth. There is not the slightest possibility of fraud." The ointment which Dr. Seidl used was the most harmless he employs in his practice.

Gradually the wounds deepened, and on Good Friday of 1927 they penetrated the hands and were visible in the palms. From the Feast of the Ascension of that year until the Good Friday of 1928, these wounds did not bleed, but blood continued to flow from Therese's eyes and from the side-wound each Friday during the ecstatic visions of the Passion, excepting for the octave of the Assumption and on the anniversary of the Little Flower's death, in 1927. On the anniversary of the death of Saint Thérèse the Passion vision had begun, but after the first picture had presented itself, the voice of the Saint was heard by the stigmatist, telling her that she would not have to suffer any more on this day, but not to receive visitors until noon.

Of the appearance of the wounds in the palms of

Therese's hands and the soles of her feet, Baron Aretin, whom we have already quoted, has written as follows: "My guide (Dr. Wutz) could observe the process. The girl, who is blind on Fridays (as a result of the flow of blood from her eyes) complained suddenly that someone had poured water into her palms, and upon investigation one saw that it was blood. At the same time, the wounds of the feet had broken through the soles. Therese herself did not see this change until Saturday. On the back of the hands and feet the stigmata are blackish, incrusted spots about the size of a ten-pfennig piece,[10] on the other side they are somewhat smaller and more reddish. They are in the highest degree sensitive to the touch. On Thursday evenings they lose their hardness and become more like fresh wounds. I have not seen the hand-wounds bleed, not even on Fridays, but those of the feet, in contrast to their previous condition, have of late begun to yield some blood. Despite the shy reluctance of Resl, lest these sacred marks be made the objects of curiosity, I have seen them so often and at such close range that there can be no doubt as to their nature.

"The gaping wound of the breast is on the left side, in which it differs from that of Christ. ... How deep this wound is, it is impossible now to determine. During the first months after its appearance it seemed to be quite flat, but recently it has apparently deepened very much, so that the girl has the feeling that it must soon be visible through her heart and on her back! This deepening was sudden. As I was told, it took place this year (1927) on the day on which the Church solemnizes the Feast of the Sacred Heart.

"A crown of eight wounds on the back of her head makes it necessary for the sufferer to wear a headcloth constantly. In normal circumstances there is nothing about her eyes of any significance to the layman." (I saw the wounds of the hands, and those of the feet partially, at the closest range when, on August 26, 1927, I was permitted to be present for four and one-half hours during Therese's ecstasy of the Passion.—*Author.*)

We must not fail to count among Therese Neumann's stigmata the bloody tears which are peculiar to her case. They begin to flow when the Friday ecstasy begins and after a few hours her cheeks and chin are covered with a thick crust of black blood, while new red tears continue to flow from the eyes and drop down. The tears appear only during the ecstasies, that is, when Therese is in a state of absolute passivity of the will; and their symbolic meaning is, it seems to me, a terrible warning to our age, which is not only estranged from God, but actually inimical to Him.

THE MARKS OF THE WOUNDS

Consternation followed the news that the marks of the Sacred Wounds of Christ had been bestowed upon Therese Neumann. This was true, at first, of Konnersreuth and the immediate vicinity only. But as early as May 7, 1926, a newspaper of Saxony printed the first report, written by a Protestant who, "in spite of many doubts, which he was unable to master," visited Therese. In her parents' house he met "the parish priest, a friendly gentleman, who complied with our request to see the invalid, but at the same time besought us not to encourage the public to come to Konnersreuth, as the sufferer's condition demanded that she be spared as much as possible."[11]

Father Naber himself had concluded his report to a newspaper with these words: "I should like to request most earnestly that visits to the invalid, particularly those of some length, be omitted: She has not taken any solid food for more than three years, and as a result of this and of the heavy loss of blood, she is so weak that rest is imperative. Besides, she wishes most of all to be let alone."[12]

The visitor from Saxony whom we have quoted, continues his narrative: "By means of a narrow stairs we gained the attic room in which Therese Neumann lies in a very simple bed. A few farmers and several women stand about the bed in the little, low-ceilinged room, and reluctantly leave at the priest's request. The girl in the bed thanks us in a friendly manner when we greet her and upon her pale countenance there is a smile. Her head is framed in a white cloth bound over her hair. She has regular teeth, but those of the upper set are defective. ... On a small table is a tiny bowl. It is the vessel from which she drinks. Once a day it is filled, says the elderly woman, who is her mother. ... At my request I am permitted to see the wounds of the hands and feet. They are now, after having been open for fourteen days, covered with a thin membrane and all of them look alike. Can human hands produce such wounds? One doubts and stands helpless in the presence of enigmas."

Are they really enigmas? For those outside of the Church they are, for us who are Catholics they are not. For us, the intelligence illumined by faith solves such riddles without difficulty. And the spirit of the Church explains, in the simplest manner, the reason for such extraordinary phenomena.

When stigmata, in the light of certain prerequisites which we shall consider later, have been certified as coming from God, they are numbered among the charismata, the exceptional gifts of grace which the Almighty bestows when He pleases, upon whom He wills. One may be saintly, that is, in the state of sanctifying grace, without possessing them; and one may have them and not be declared a saint by the Church. For Heaven is populated by many more than the small number of saints who are officially recognized as such. Although of the more than 300 stigmatists, only 60 have thus far been raised to the honors of the altar, that is, canonized, this fact does not mean that the others were not worthy of canonization. It means simply that thus far neither the diocesan authorities nor the religious order to which they belonged has initiated the process by which Rome might eventually proclaim them blessed and saints.

Those outside the Church stand helpless before such questions as these: What is the purpose of the stigmatization? Why does God bestow the stigmata? Our answer shall take the form of a counter-query: What purpose did Our Lord have when He worked miracles? He knew man, for whose sake He became man; He knew that among men were some who would accept His word at once, without question. Nathaniel was one of them, one of the exceptions. Even among His chosen ones, His apostles, there was a Thomas; and there were many others who did not believe Him. These, too, He wished to win and to save, all of those to whom He said, "Unless you see signs and wonders, you believe not." (John 4:48.) He does not turn away from them. He does not say to them, If you will not believe, go your way! No, He wishes to bring all to faith in Him; and therefore, out of love for the incredulous, he performs miracles. (1 Cor. 14:22.) He works wonders that they may believe in Him, and follow Him in His Kingdom, the Church which He is to establish. As many of His words testify, it was not only to restore a single invalid to health, but to induce unbelievers and doubters to have faith that He performed miracles. By means of that which their senses could perceive, they were to be won for the truth, the Church, and faith, so that God's glory might be increased and spread among men. By His works they were to know Him, by them be brought to knowledge and adoration. And are the charismata other than miracles? Does not Saint Paul speak of them? Consider his first letter to the Corinthians. In it, how briefly and concisely, he declares that they are of the Holy Ghost, *ad utilitatem*, for the benefit not of the recipient only, but also that of others. They are evidences of the existence of God and of the truth of His revelation. They compel the thinking man to acknowledge a supernatural order and to accept all that necessarily follows from such an acknowledgment.

God makes use of visible signs and wonders that they may be seen of men, that through them and for men's sake, the truth may be recognized. In each of His miracles there is the element of the much-despised sensation, the direct appeal to the senses, the natural means with which to draw those who do not believe. He makes use of the senses to draw the incredulous. He operates through sensations, through the "impossible" to overcome them: "Indeed this was the Son of God!" (Matt, 27:54.) The Redeemer might have performed His miracles in secret, but that is exactly what He did not wish to do. He stood in the market place of life, He intentionally exposed His divinely miraculous deeds to the public gaze and profane curiosity. "If I had not done among them," He said, "the works that no other man hath done, they would not have sin; but now they have both seen and hated both Me and My Father." (John 15:24.) He endured the onrush of the throngs which followed Him because of His miracles, so that only flight or the night remained to Him for prayer. And He declared explicitly: "If I do not the works of My Father, believe Me not. But if I do, though you will not believe Me, believe the works; that you may know and believe that the Father is in Me, and I in the Father." (John 10:37-38.)

Our Lord walks no more in our midst; He has returned
to His heavenly Father. But He is still, in accordance with
His holy promise, with us, with His, the Catholic, Church,
and will continue to be until the end of time. He is,
therefore, with us in this year of grace. And where He is
we must see traces of Him and of His characteristic acts,
miracles. There are, in our days, many miracles, the
number of them far greater than the world imagines, and
we shall tell of them in a book which will soon appear.
Now, however, we shall consider the stigmata only.

In this age of the radio, the automobile, the cinema, and
the airplane, it is indeed an alien tongue, a strange
language in which Konnersreuth speaks to the world's
new pagans. "In other tongues and other lips I will speak
to this people." (1 Cor. 14:21.) Paul reminds us of these
words of God. Today it is the strange speech of the
bleeding and crucified Redeemer which is addressed to us
through Therese Neumann. Not she speaks, but the God
Whom she serves. If this were not so, the Church would
long since have pronounced a verdict of unmistakable
severity. Father Naber would long ere this have ceased to
be Therese's spiritual director. A bolt of lightning would
have been released by Rome.

First of all, what does the Church say concerning the
stigmata?

They have been known to her since the days of
primitive Christianity. The Apostle Paul, who described
himself as one crucified with Christ and his message to
men as a revelation from Jesus Christ, closes his letter to
the Galatians thus: "... for I bear the marks of the Lord
Jesus in my body."[13] After him, at least so far as our
knowledge goes, this exceptional gift of grace seems not to
have been bestowed upon anyone until he appeared of

whom it has been said that none other was so like unto the crucified Saviour—the glorious Saint Francis of Assisi. The bestowal of the stigmata upon him was an event of such high significance in her history that the Church established a special feast to commemorate it forever in the liturgy. On this feast, September 17, the Church places these words, as the first prayer of the Mass, upon the lips of her priests: *"Domine Jesu Christe, qui frigescente mundo, ad inflammandum corda nostra tui amoris in carne beatissimi Patris Nostri Francisci passionis tuae sacra Stigmata renovasti, concede propitius...* (O Lord Jesus Christ, Who, when the world grew cold, didst renew the sacred marks of Thy passion in the flesh of the most blessed Francis, to inflame our hearts with the fire of Thy love, graciously grant...)

But the world, which had been warmed by the ardor of the Poverello, became lukewarm again and cold in its faith in the Crucified and His work, the Church. Heresies led many to apostasy from the Church, then to denial of Christ as the Son of God, and finally their descendants sank into a new paganism, so that it was as though the Saviour had never come. Therefore, God worked new wonders to remind these stray sheep again and again that He is both the Living God of eternal life and the Redeemer Who became man and suffered and died for all generations, as they follow one upon another. In His own way and using human beings as His instruments, He drew the attention of mankind back to Himself, the Crucified; to Himself and to the vessel of salvation which He established, the Catholic Church. He would declare in unmistakable terms that this Church is, in the midst of the many misleading "churches" of human origin, His one, true Church. It is probable that this is the real reason why the charismata of the stigmata are found only in the Catholic Church.

Are the conditions in our days better than they were in the past? Have faith in Christ and love for Him increased in these times? Nay, they have, rather, decreased, and so Christ in His mercy has renewed the fire of His love in the flesh of favored men and women, has bestowed upon them the marks of His Sacred Wounds, in order to inflame the hearts of so many of our contemporaries, for whom also He suffered, but who do not care to know anything about Him. Saint Paul maintains that for the sake of the unbelievers, such gifts of grace are bestowed; and it is a fact that along with the thousands who came to Konnersreuth because they saw the Saviour mirrored in Therese Neumann and recognized His hand at work there, there were many who did not believe, many heretics, many doubters. Whether some of them, having come and having seen, received the gift of faith, we do not know, for we cannot see the hearts of men. It is probable that the situation is now as it was when Our Lord dwelt among us in His human form and performed miracles; some believe, but many go away still incredulous. However, at Konnersreuth this has come to pass: All have been brought face to face, in a soul-stirring manner with the fact that Christ the Son of God exists; with the fact that He *propter nos homines et propter nostram salutem...* (for us men and for our salvation) suffered and was crucified and died. And as a believing Catholic, I deem it an exceedingly great grace that I have been permitted to see the fact of the Redemption, which took place in the gray antiquity of two thousand years ago, renewed as a personal experience. And numerous testimonials in the press show that I am but one of many.

That, then, is the purpose of the charismata of the Sacred Wounds. The purpose is not to give opportunity for experiments to a group of unbelieving professors, so that they may construct new theories, new denials that the soul exists. They ought to declare, honestly, when they reach the borderland between the natural and the supernatural: This is the boundary of our field of work in the sensible perception of facts, and therefore also the confines of our science. Beyond this, *ignoramus,* we do not know. In this connection, a non-Catholic has written very aptly: "The competence of medicine in this case must be disputed. The verdict of the medical expert has no value, because he does not touch the determining fact. For it is a question not of a medical, but of a religious phenomenon. And as such it is the fruit of Catholicism and is within the province of the Church, which does well in guarding and cherishing it."[14]

ORIGIN OF THE STIGMATA

The appearance of the stigmata on the body of Therese Neumann had the effect which is usual in such cases. The stigmata were discussed with embittered vehemence; their origin became the subject of agitated controversy, as did also their genuineness. In this age of the press it was inevitable that the daily newspapers should at once engage in the battle and convey the news thereof to hundreds of thousands, even millions, throughout Europe and far beyond. It is no exaggeration to say that Therese Neumann and Konnersreuth became, quite suddenly, objects of interest to half of the population of the world. The universal interest in this matter proves the innate persistent preoccupation of men with the questions of a personal God and a supernatural world. Though there was, at first, no more than a query as to the possibility of a supernatural phenomenon, the news from Konnersreuth gripped the souls of men.

What is the origin of the stigmata borne by Therese Neumann?

There is a limited number of possible answers.

First of all, are they of natural or supernatural origin?

If their origin is natural, that is, in conformity with the laws of nature, they must be due either to *deception*, intentional and artificial causation of the wounds; or they are the result of *disease*.

If the stigmata are of supernatural origin, there are also two possibilities. Their production is either *demoniacal* or *divine*.

CAN IT BE DECEPTION?

The position of the Church in the Neumann case may be gauged by the attitude of the parish priest of Konnersreuth, the Reverend Father Naber. He represents for Therese the divine authority bestowed upon His Church by Jesus Christ. Father Naber remains to this day the conscientiously careful spiritual director of this child of his flock, and he vouches with all his personal as well as his ecclesiastical authority for the irreproachable character and unimpeachable conduct of Therese Neumann. He continues to enjoy the unlimited confidence of his superiors of the Diocese of Regensburg, whom he has from the beginning supplied with detailed reports. He has been parish priest at Konnersreuth for more than twenty years and is highly respected throughout the parish and in the entire district. A cultured, distinguished gentleman, of deep piety, he is an ardent client of St. Francis de Sales, whose spirit he has imbibed. Thousands know him, have seen him, and observed him. Of the many estimates we shall quote a few.

"The first visit was to the interesting parish priest," says a Swiss writer. "With his intelligent, critical, humorously smiling eyes, he reminds you at once of the venerable chaplain of the hospital at Lucerne. There lies upon his countenance that look of candor and truth which is the brightest adornment of every priest in our own country."[15]

"The parish priest, a lovable, friendly man, who inspires confidence at first sight, is himself, most of all, astounded at the strange things of which he has been the witness. 'Why has all this happened among us?' is his amazed question."[16]

"The village priest is much too competent and critical to warrant the least suspicion that he might be accessory to any deception."[17]

"...The venerable priest is completely convinced that it is a matter of supernatural origin. There can be no question of fraud or deception, or of the dark realm of hysteria. I believe he would go through fire in defense of the truth of his conviction. He has known Therese Neumann since her school days."[18]

"Father Naber, one might say, shares the life of Therese Neumann hour by hour. It would be ridiculous to consider any basic phantasy on his part. It is for him not a matter of theology at all, but of simple faith which nothing can disturb. He is completely absorbed in the experiences which have come upon him, so to speak, over night."[19]

"Near the church, in the midst of a crowd of clergymen and members of the laity, stands the parish priest. His is an exceptionally spiritual face, framed in gray hair. ... A look into his pure and gentle face tells all who have learned to read human countenances, that any notion of pious deception is out of the question. ... The clergyman—one ought to emphasize this fact—honestly endeavors to prevent any unseemly exploitation of the phenomenon, and to distinguish truth from fiction, faith from superstition."[20]

"The venerable parish priest makes an impression utterly different from that of a manager or a businesslike impresario, or of an ambitious country pastor who desires to see his parish the object of pilgrimages and one of his parishioners proclaimed a saint."[21]

"Both the parents, who are simple village folk, and the worthy parish priest ... make an impression which inspires complete confidence. ... It is wholly false to say that the relatives or the priest or even the stigmatist herself, as some newspapers have said, endeavor to exploit the singular occurrences."[22]

The estimates of Therese's parents on the part of those who have seen them and spoken with them, are uniformly favorable, though in many of the reports one encounters complaints made by them that the steady stream of humanity causes constant inconvenience and increases the difficulty of their labors.[23] Unanimous, too, is the testimony of the reports that neither her parents, nor Therese, accept even one pfennig from any of the thousands of visitors, despite many attempts to force money upon them. We shall see, later, why those concerned do not forbid visitors. At any rate, there is not the least motive for fraud.

A throng of tens of thousands has visited Konnersreuth during the last year and a half and Therese Neumann has been the cynosure of searching glances; but not a single voice has been heard to suggest even the possibility of fraud, of an intentional deception; or, as the common expression is, a swindle. Such charges are, significantly, met with in publications which, avoiding even the semblance of personal investigation, have the instinctive impression that Therese Neumann is the source of dire peril to their cause, which is to combat all positive belief in God. When one reads the falsehoods and slanders which these papers employ it would seem as though hell itself were in tumult, gnashing its teeth in rage at its own impotence.[24]

In contrast with such base methods, many eyewitnesses, among them adherents of other than the Catholic Church, and such as are beyond any suspicion of favoritism toward the Church, have been honest and courageous enough to proclaim their convictions. Here are a few examples:

"Whoever observes the occurrences at Konnersreuth with unbiased eyes must admit that the stigmatization of Therese Neumann is not a fraud, but a fact which cannot be denied. The wounds are there, they can be seen by all, and they bleed or have bled."[25]

"I am thoroughly convinced that one cannot do the girl a graver injustice than to accuse her of intentional autosuggestion, or even of conscious hallucination."[26]

"At all events, the naturalness, simplicity, calmness, and ingenuousness of Therese Neumann have made an impression which neither my companion and I nor any of the other visitors could withstand. ... No, positively no, I said to myself more emphatically each minute, this 28-year-old daughter of Tailor Neumann of Konnersreuth, the eldest of ten children, the former stable-maid, who has never yet caused grief to her father or mother, is not guilty of fraud."[27]

"To her physician, who spoke of an hysterical trauma, she put the pointed question, frankly: 'Tell me, am I really a fraud?' and his answer was an emphatic 'No!' "[28]

"The natural candor of her spirit is probably one reason

why, of the many thousands who have been witnesses of the remarkable happenings, not one has dared to say that the girl is guilty of deception. On the contrary, there has been in all reports thus far a singular unanimity to the effect that such an assumption is utterly ridiculous."[29]

"One would do the girl a grave injustice if one were to say that the phenomena are the result of deception on her part."[30]

"The parish priest of Münchenreuth offered one thousand marks to any one producing evidence which would prove that the stigmatization at Konnersreuth is a fraud or even a deception. Thus far no bold knight has entered the list to win this considerable prize."[31]

"Skepticism may, despite the physical impossibility of it, resort to the word fraud. In the chain of events which I have narrated, and which are worlds apart from any fraud, even the keenest mistrust must see how subordinate is this complementary phenomenon (the abstinence from food); much too minor to engage the attention of fraud, wholly apart from the fact that the Therese Neumann whom I have the honor and good fortune to know, is infinitely above such petty suspicions."[32]

"I do not believe there is fraud. Not only because the girl made the most favorable impression possible upon me—and I admit that I, too, might have been deceived—but also because she has for a long time been subject to the authority of the Catholic clergy."[33]

"I declare emphatically that I consider an intentional deception out of the question."[34]

"First of all, any suspicion of intentional fraud is to be dismissed. The phenomena are genuine; many of them appear before the eyes of witnesses. In particular, the stigmata are genuine."[35]

Because she strives so conscientiously to report and

reproduce with absolute fidelity what she sees in her Passion-ecstasies, Therese Neumann is sensitive toward charges of unreliability. She is capable, in this matter, of some heat, and an investigation of her trustworthiness must yield a verdict in her favor. But her attitude toward the personal charge of fraud is reflected in a statement which Dr. Hollnsteiner reports as follows: "Do you know (said Therese) that I like him who tells me in the morning that I am a fraud just as much as the one who tells me in the evening that I am a saint? I am sorry for both of them, because of their stupidity. The one is stupid because he believes such things can be 'invented'; the other because he doesn't seem to know that, while all of us hope to be saints some day, we are a long way from it as yet."

ARE THE STIGMATA THE RESULT OF DISEASE?

Are the stigmata outward signs of an inner malady? Our answer to this question shall again be a counter-query: Are there Catholic diseases? Are there sicknesses to which a man is prone because of his *Weltanschauung*, his philosophy of life? Every man of medicine will deny that this is true. But it is a fact that history knows not a single non-Catholic who has received genuine stigmata. All the stigmatists, men and women, have been Catholics. And this despite the fact that there are, outside of the Church, people of deep and upright spirituality whose sole aim in life is to conform to the will of God, insofar as they know it, and by their conduct please Him. According to Catholic doctrine, such people belong to the soul of the Church, though they are not formally members of it. But more than 300 known cases of stigmatization show that membership in the Church is a prerequisite. If this is true, the disease which produces the stigmata must be exclusively and peculiarly a Catholic disease.

Why do many take it for granted that stigmatization is pathological? Because wounds are usually symptoms of disease and (apart from injury) cannot be explained naturally in any other way; because stigmatists, experience shows, undergo a preparatory period of suffering; and finally, because many refuse to recognize God as the Giver of any gifts whatsoever.

The accounts of Therese Neumann's stigmata which have thus far appeared in the daily newspapers and in magazines, have been amazingly superficial. Nowhere do we meet with references to even a few other cases of stigmatization and a thorough consideration of them as a means of comparison with that of Konnersreuth. One mentions, perhaps, a few unimportant details in the life of Anna Catherine Emmerich; cites a few other names, and informs one's readers that Dr. Imbert-Gourbeyre in his book, *La Stigmatisation*, counts the bearers of the wound-marks at 321, of which number 41 were men. Another name is mentioned, occasionally, that of the stigmatized Pater Pio da Pietrelcina, and it is generally cited incorrectly, as P. Pietro. Louise Lateau is merely mentioned, and the other stigmatists of our days, such as Elena Ajello, Barbara Pfister, Sister Mary of Jesus Crucified, Gemma Galgani—of these one does not seem to know even the names. But it is particularly the cases of the last two named which destroy the contention that stigmatization is the result of disease, for both of them received the marks of the Wounds while enjoying perfect health. And when the attempt is made to establish a causal connection, in the case of Therese Neumann, between the cessation of the periods (for more than five years past) and the stigmata, we place in opposition to such an assertion the fact that there have been forty-one male stigmatists.

According to the laws of nature, each disease has exterior manifestations, symptoms. In regard to the stigmata, there is a basic, essential uniformity as to the places in which they appear; namely, where Christ bore His wounds. Exceptions have been noted. As with Therese Neumann, so with other stigmatists, the heart-wound sometimes appears on the left instead of the right side, in which the lance pierced the Redeemer's breast. But whether on the right side or the left, the objective is the same: the wounding of the heart. On the other hand, stigmatization is so varied that thus far I have not come upon two cases in which the qualities of the wounds were in all aspects identical. In some instances all of the five wounds are visible, in other instances a smaller number. Some stigmata are always visible, others only periodically. Sometimes they are entirely invisible, but recognizable by touch, as with Sister Mary Fidelis Weiss (who died at Reutberg in Upper Bavaria in 1923). Changes are, however, always closely connected with the liturgical calendar. The wounds borne by Pater Pio of the Capuchin Order remained unchanged, whereas those of Gemma Galgani (1903) appeared during two years on Thursday nights at eight o'clock and disappeared after three o'clock on Friday afternoons; and their appearance was unaccompanied by any preparation, pain, or feeling of pressure. The side-wound of this stigmatist bled continuously. In her case ecstasies came later.

If the stigmata are symptoms of disease, all stigmatists would, of necessity, be victims of the same disease, the one which has this effect. An examination of the sufferings of the stigmatists (including those which preceded the bestowal of the marks) shows that their maladies were not unknown, mysterious, indefinable ones, but such as constantly assail thousands of their fellow men, without producing a single stigma in any of these thousands. Therese's sicknesses were such as her physician was well acquainted with, and yet the stigmata appeared! It is to be noted, too, that the preliminary sicknesses are of the most varied kinds. How then could they produce, in all instances, the same effects? How could they cause exactly the same results in exactly the same organs? This contradicts the natural law that similar causes have similar effects. It can be maintained, therefore, that there is no known sickness which produces stigmatization.

We might ask a further question: What disease is it which causes open but not incrusted, not festering wounds that bleed only on specific days of the Church calendar; wounds which defy every attempt at medical treatment, which instead of being cured, cause the bearer intense pain when remedies are applied? Are they, perhaps, a verification, a confirmation of the words of the Voice to Therese: "No physician shall be able to help you"?

And what is the name of the disease which produces these symptoms after a seven-years' abstinence from solid food, and three years' abstinence from liquid food, without disintegration of the body?

Let us repeat that it is not fair to pick out one or another factor or incident and disregard all other circumstances or incidents in the case. All of them together constitute the phenomena of Therese Neumann, and all of them must be given due consideration at the same time.

ARE THE STIGMATA DUE TO HYSTERIA?

A non-Catholic publication in Berlin has written: "Well, if one who is hysterical can live for eight months more than six years without partaking of food, we are inclined to say to science, Pray, how can we, too, become hysterical?"[36] No learned man who has thus far written about hysteria, has dared to assert that it consists in complete and voluntary abstinence from food during a period of several years without bringing physical collapse in its wake. However, let us turn our attention again specifically to the stigmata and their origin. Here again it is true that one cannot be satisfied with saying, they may be explained in this manner or in that one, or in some other way. The question is, How did they actually originate on the person of Therese Neumann? The answer to this question has not yet been given. There have been speculations, attempts at explanation, and we shall consider them in the next chapter. But hysteria? "Of course, ... hysteria, autosuggestion, suggestion from without ...," says W. von Weisl, M. D., an Israelite, "Glorious explanation, which by using a number of unusual words does not make an inexplicable matter plain."[37] "... I refuse to acknowledge hysteria as an explanation. The word hysteria may be a diagnosis, but it is no explanation."[38]

"It is now clear that the catchword 'hysteria' must be discarded. Experts in psychiatry and theology have declared that it will not help us to deal with the case scientifically," says Dr. Hollnsteiner. "The symptoms of hysteria, such as abnormal emotionalism, insistent egotism, pathological lying, etc., are altogether absent. Only in one direction have I discovered a certain anxiety on the part of Therese Neumann, and that is, lest she tell what is not absolutely true. More than once she returned to what had been said, in order to clarify what might possibly have been misinterpreted; or she would state frankly that she could no longer remember with complete certainty this or that detail."[39]

"Let it be said, once for all," writes Baron von Aretin, who has observed Therese for days and has spoken with her, "that the most thorough medical examination ... by the Erlanger commission established the fact that there is not present even a suspicion of the condition which is summed up by the word 'hysteria,' but that her critical love of the truth deserves special mention."[40]

"I avoid the word 'hysteria,' which has more than one meaning in science and in the popular mind stands for psychical conditions which do not obtain in this case," says Dr. R. Reissmann,[41] who is by no means adverse to phantastic explanations. And a member of a religious order declares that "equipped with all the experiences and memories of one who has for years had a spiritual director's care of women suffering from hysteria, I entered the little room on the alert to detect the least indication of anything which would permit a natural explanation of the phenomena. But I must confess that I was completely defeated. There was nothing abnormal, none of the sentimental excesses which one encounters so often among invalid women."[42] A priest, Dr. Martin Mayr, gives his impression as follows: "A child of the village, Therese, like Saint Francis of Assisi, loves nature. She plays with her turtledoves, which at her command stop their cooing; her two canary birds give her pleasure, as do her flowers and the two little fish in an aquarium. She is anything but hysterical. ... Any man who says that this peasant girl of clear understanding and sound judgment is hysterical, either does not know the signs of hysteria or has never heard Therese's hearty, joyous laughter."[43]

And I, who was privileged to spend many hours in the

presence of Therese Neumann, can corroborate what these witnesses have written. Her quiet friendliness, her natural, unaffected simplicity, her genuine desire to remain in the background, her implicit obedience to ecclesiastical authority, and, most important of all, the fact that her concern is least of all with herself, but chiefly with the Saviour and the needs of strangers—all these circumstances are voices speaking distinctly in favor of Therese Neumann and against her detractors, against doubters.

The last testimonial shall be that of a Swiss whose abhorrence of all "hysterical women" could be overcome only by the pressure of friendliness before he would consent to make the detour which took him to Konnersreuth. He attributed "the most common form of stigmatization to hysteria and autosuggestion," but after visiting Therese Neumann he wrote:

"After almost a half hour of the torture of questions, my companion, who had listened to all of the conversation with the keenest of attention, felt his heart stirred to keenest sympathy. So when I began to joke heartily with the sorely bothered Therese, and she entered good humoredly into the bantering, my companion recovered his composure. Resl spoke entirely in the local dialect, and at first it was not readily understandable. When I said, 'Now, Resl, if you keep on talking in that way, I shall use the dialect of my country, and then neither of us shall understand what the other says,' she laughed heartily and said, 'Your Reverence, I talk as I can.' The hospitable parish priest suggests that we have a third glass of beer. I asked, jestingly, 'What do you say to that, Resl?' Her answer was, 'Well, your Reverence, if it is sure not to be too much, go ahead and have another glass.' ... 'Resl, you are a rascally saint.' ... 'No, no, no, not a saint. I am only doing what I believe is my duty. I'd much rather work, but if the dear

God wills it this way, why it is all the same to me.' ... 'You haven't prayed at all this afternoon, not even a single Our Father for your tormenters.' ... 'Oh, there have been worse tormenters here. As to praying, I believe you are right. It is well to pray. But I am no *Betschwester*.[44] In the morning I go to church. In the afternoon I like to go into the woods or sit under a tree in the meadow and look at the beauty of nature. I like especially to hear the birds. And every little flower and every star is a miracle of God's and lifts our thoughts to Him.' "[45]

This priest closes his observation with an emphatic statement in favor of the character of Therese and the genuineness of her stigmata, and declares that there is no question of hysteria or autosuggestion, unless, indeed, the whole world is hysterical and no human being can any longer maintain that he is normal.[46]

IS AUTOSUGGESTION THE CAUSE?

Most of the attempts to explain the stigmatization of Therese Neumann in a natural way are based on the charge that the wounds are caused by an hallucination; that they arise from autosuggestion, an extraordinary gift of phantasy in connection with exceptional will power and the influence of environment.

We dealt with this matter briefly in connection with the third cure. Now that we are considering the stigmata, we shall give it a more thorough attention.

In suggestion and hypnotism it is another's will which is imposed; in autosuggestion and autohypnotism it is one's own will which forces a creation of its own imagination upon the ego. In any event, the will must be operative, and indeed, operative in a specially potent manner. Without the will neither suggestion nor autosuggestion is possible. We do not deny that autosuggestion, that is, the involuntary reception of a given possibility, is capable of eliciting great activity within human beings; but they do not, generally, lie in the direction in which the will is bent. I can, for instance, imagine that I have won 50,000 marks in the lottery, and I can keep on imagining this until I believe it. The result, however, will be a keen disappointment, melancholia perhaps, or insanity, but never that, because of my strong phantasy in connection with my will, I really get the 50,000 marks.

Of the thousands who came to Konnersreuth, only one made the discovery that Therese Neumann was the victim of hypnosis, that a force outside of herself, the will of another is operative. This one saw Therese in the Passion-ecstasy and wrote:

"I was permitted to remain longer than the others. What imposed itself upon me more forcefully than all else was that throughout the time of suffering, a priest with markedly sharp features, standing motionless at the foot of the bed, gazed steadfastly at her ... and had the medium in his power. ... Nobody could, or wished to tell me who he was."[47]

Did this mysterious unknown individual then stand at Therese's bed during each ecstasy from Thursday evening till Friday noon, throughout the years of her suffering in order to stare at her and have her in his power? More than a hundred thousand people who have seen Therese in her Friday agonies can testify that the "priest with markedly sharp features" did not stand at the foot of the bed nor anywhere else. The only man whom the description and the time could possibly fit, and who on this particular

Friday actually did stand at the foot of the bed, is one of
my dearest friends, and at the time he was still a Protestant
minister.

The suspicion that there is autohypnosis; that is, that
Therese Neumann hypnotizes herself and that the stigmata
originated in this manner, is cast aside by the man who
expressed it. He did not, of course, take the trouble to find
out whether or not Therese really did hypnotize herself.
He says: "The hypnotic concentration upon the vision of
the crucified Saviour *might* have such a physiological
effect upon the capillary system, which, as has been shown
lately, undergoes changes when there is no more than a
mere strain of attention." But "this explanation is not
sufficient, for the wounds caused by hypnosis have the
characteristics of normal wounds and heal rather normally,
while the stigmata are physiological puzzles because they
do not fester nor heal, nor respond to any sort of
treatment. I doubt, too, whether so great an organic change
as the creation of the heart-wound can be achieved
through autosuggestion alone."[48]

So we come to autosuggestion, the favorite refuge of
those who seek a natural explanation. Several of these
explanations are before us. Not one of them endeavors to
give an *objective* presentation of the essential prerequisites,
in order to investigate the phenomena and determine that
the interior prerequisites actually exist. In particular her
religious life and its development are mysteries to these
learned men.

One of the visitors sees a predisposition, an inciting
tendency in Therese's "devotion to the Passion," in her
"flirtatious," "coquettish" attitude toward suffering as the
chief requisite for gaining God's favor. "The story of the
Passion gripped her in girlhood especially, in the church
hang the Stations, and near the village on a hill stand the

three crosses; in the room is a little altar with a crucifix on the wall and a statue of the Sacred Heart. The catechism, and literature dealing with Thérèse of the Infant Jesus, bound her mental horizon. Therefore, I believe that if her prayer, that is, her will, her concentration, were directed away from the Passion and from ecstasy, she might be freed; I believe in the possibility that a sojourn in a secular hospital, in an entirely different environment, might influence her so that the bleeding, possibly the stigmata, too, would disappear."[49]

This non-Catholic seems to be a total stranger to Catholic life. When our first catechist, the Rev. Father Schiessl at Munich, told us the story of the Passion for the first time, we sixty boys wept unrestrainedly, and the teacher was compelled to weep with us. The Stations hang in hundreds of thousands of Catholic churches, and millions of Catholics "pray the Stations." Wayside crosses meet the traveler at almost every step in Catholic lands. Home altars and *Herrgottswinkeln* with crucifixes are not peculiar to the home of Therese Neumann, but are to be found in almost every Catholic house, as are also statues of the Sacred Heart; and there is scarcely a member of the Church who does not own a prayer book. In all of these there is nothing at all unusual. It is rather the rule. The exception is Therese Neumann herself, who despite her normally Catholic environment, developed in an abnormally Catholic manner.

What does Therese herself say to the charge of autosuggestion? A letter of July 2, 1926, gives us this account: "Some liberalistic people wished to convince Therese that the stigmata were to be traced to her imagination. They questioned her frankly and said to her: 'Because you meditate with such intensity upon the Sacred Wounds of the Divine Saviour, they finally appeared on

your body, too.' Then she made this answer: 'Well, then if I meditated on the devil, I would gradually grow horns.' "
There is no retort for such logic. It might remind us, at least, that idle ladies of our days meditate daily upon the ideal of beauty and concentrate upon it all the will power they possess in the form of a desire to conform to it. But I do not know of even a single case, though this is a simple matter and does not concern the stigmata, in which this meditation, this concentration of will power has been effective. On the contrary, the longer the meditation and concentration last, the more rouge and face cream and a hundred other cosmetics must be applied in order to forestall, apparently, the impending doom. Let a scientist produce a drop of blood through autosuggestion. It has not been done and we are still waiting for the verification of such a fact by witnesses. The stigmata of Therese Neumann exist, and dozens of written testimonials are at all times available.

Another construes the process according to his own ideas, without giving consideration to the facts in the case. "The imagination of the blind girl could not busy itself with anything but the legends of the saints which were occasionally read to her. She had never seen any pictures other than those in books of devotion and the deeply impressive Passion scenes of her village church. To this were added the consoling example of compulsory suffering and the conviction that suffering is holy. Such a robust peasant maid had to transform her pain into the will-to-suffer, she 'lived into' the Passion of the Redeemer, into the manner of His suffering. His wounds became her wounds. Moody religious meditation without freshening and distracting activity was inevitable because of her suffering."[50]

All this is merely presumption, but not proof. We shall,

for the present, confine ourselves to stating that the first stigma, the heart-wound, came as a result of the first ecstatic vision. The subject of the vision was the Saviour in the Garden of Olives, a vision of Him *before* His side was pierced. Therefore, no matter how intensely Therese saw and shared what she saw; no matter how strongly the vision was impressed upon her, her wound was not His wound.

※※※

No autosuggestion is possible without activity of the will. But not even ordinary action of the will is sufficient. It has been said that "by means of a special intensification of her will power, the invalid manages to receive bleeding wounds." Let us suppose that in her solitude (during her long invalidism) she devoted all her spiritual powers through the years toward this single goal: to achieve the stigmata of Christ. Finally the wounds appear, and they will not respond to any remedies. This is evidence of a most extraordinary force of will. It would not, however, exclude a theological explanation "... that Therese Neumann in possessing such will power is one among hundreds of millions of human beings."[51]

First of all, let us remember that for more than twenty years Therese has been under the spiritual direction of her parish priest and confessor, the Reverend Father Naber, who has testified most emphatically to her complete docility and her exemplary obedience in spiritual matters. No Catholic priest permits himself to be guided in such a case by any sort of inclination to mysticism, but solely by the Church's regulations concerning the care of souls. He would seek diligently to prevent hallucination, phantastic excesses, mysticism, brooding, flirtation with suffering. He

would forbid his charge to indulge in them. Father Naber
would have done so, if it had been necessary. Like all other
priests, he knows full well the perils of the imagination and
of self-love. He studied pastoral theology at the seminary.
Autosuggestion meets its most relentless foe in the father
confessor, who insists upon relentlessly rooting out even
the intimation of it. Therese has obeyed Father Naber, not
unwillingly, but gladly, as an obedient child. He has guided
her as he guided his other spiritual children, as millions of
Catholics who have not the stigmata, are guided by their
priests. He presented the Saviour to her as a solace in her
suffering; he counseled submission to the will of God, and
she acquiesced at once. At this point there is a parting of
the ways. It is the boundary beyond which autosuggestion
becomes an utter impossibility. Catholic mysticism is
governed by specific laws, and its beginning is abnegation.
If Therese had refused to subject her will, unconditionally
and whole-heartedly, to the Divine Will, she would not
have been able to pass through the gate on which is
inscribed the petition of the Our Father: Thy will be done!
This gate is the only one which leads to the spiritual
ascent. Father Ginhac, S.J., who himself trod the way of
perfection successfully, has written: "Not great things
bring the reward of Paradise. The soul must not say, I wish
to suffer, I wish this trial or humiliation, or that
renunciation; for self-will spoils it all. ... The essential
thing is to accept with love and complete conformity with
God's will whatever He may send. There are souls in hell
who desired trials and humiliation. God answered their
petitions but they did not take advantage of these graces.
Their pride caused their downfall. We must accept
everything without desiring, grateful for what God sends."

All the statements which Therese has made agree in
this, that she is actually and wholly submissive to the will

of God. There still sound in my ears the words she uttered repeatedly: "As the dear Saviour wills. It is all the same to me." She does not say, "I wish to suffer, send me what I desire." She says only, "Whatever is Thy will is my will, too; whether it be health or sickness, life or death. I desire nothing but what Thou desirest me to have, though I do not know what Thy will is." In such circumstances it would be a monstrous thing, and inconceivable on the part of Therese Neumann, to say, Lord, I desire the marks of Thy wounds! For graces cannot be demanded. They flow only from the sovereign will of God. When my companion at Konnersreuth, a priest of long experience as a director of souls, said to Therese, "Resl, the worst is still to come; it will come soon, very soon. It is the night of the soul, the abandonment by God. You shall call upon the Saviour and He will not answer," the stigmatist replied with utter calmness: "Whatever the dear Saviour wishes. It is all the same to me."

Therese has long since surrendered her own will, and her attitude toward God is solely this: "Father, not my will but Thine be done!" There are many proofs of this, and not a single disproof of it. There is thus excluded, also, the possibility of hallucination, of phantasy as an explanation, and the second prerequisite of autosuggestion is shown to be wanting.

Let it be established, then, that in Therese's case the imperative prerequisites of autosuggestion are lacking. Those who assert that autosuggestion prevails, do so without reference to the facts, without consulting them at all, and their contention is an arbitrary one. There is no proof.

A solitary voice is heard making an extremely modern but therefore no less ludicrous explanation: radio! The "excess of wireless electricity (ultraviolet rays, etc.)" is to be made responsible for the "puzzling" occurrences. One wonders, are the Konnersreuth phenomena something altogether new to the man acquainted with Catholic mysticism and hagiography? How came they to have the stigmata, the 321 whom Dr. Imbert-Gourbeyre records, who lived when there was no such excess of electricity in the form of wireless waves?

ARE THE STIGMATA OF SUPERNATURAL ORIGIN?

Turning now to the second great question, "Are the stigmata of supernatural origin?", we find that there are two possibilities. The one is that their source may be demoniacal. Theology provides simple tests, based on Catholic teaching, and according to these tests Therese Neumann's stigmata are not of demoniacal origin, because she lives in complete submission to the will of God, and consequently, in submission to the authority of the Catholic Church and her representatives; and because the effect of her stigmatization has been to draw her closer to God, not farther away from Him. The devil uses self-will in man as his most effective tool. He tempts man to pride and to resistance to the authority of Jesus Christ in His Church. There is no evil spirit in voluntary obedience to the authority of the Church.

Thus we come to the last of the questions: If Therese Neumann's stigmata are of supernatural but not demoniacal origin, must not their source be divinely supernatural? And in this matter, again, the stigmata must be judged as a whole, with due attention to all factors, to the many details.

It is at once apparent that while the question of

purpose cannot be intelligently answered when a natural explanation is attempted, when a supernatural one is essayed a reasonable and logical answer is offered by the teachings of the Church. We no longer face "the riddle of Konnersreuth" but understand that we are on the solid, familiar soil on which Catholics have felt at home through two thousand years. We know there are laws, based upon the divine doctrines of Catholicism and therefore absolutely dependable, which govern these matters. Consult any Catholic guide to the spiritual life, any history of the Saints, any theological textbook, and you will find that what is taking place at Konnersreuth in our days took place many times before.

There has just been placed in my hands an old, yellowed little book entitled *Seraphische Liebes-flammen zu Ehren der gros-wunderthätig-seligen Elisabeth Bona, einer seraphischen Ordens-Tochter aus dem Löbl. der oberdeutschen Strasburger-Provinz Ord. min. Convent S. P. Francisi einverleibten Jungfrauen-Kloster Zu Reuthe in Schwaben.* (Cum approb. Sup. Printed in 1767 at Constance.) Reading from this book, it was easy to imagine that Therese Neumann speaks from its pages. Remarkably enough, this Franciscan nun, who died in 1420, bore the miraculous stigmata of Christ's wounds, and during twelve years she needed neither food nor sleep. Consider also the histories of the Syrian stigmatist, Sister Mary of Jesus Crucified, who died in 1878 and whose biography appeared in 1924; and the lovable Gemma Galgani, who died in 1903. We discover that, apart from exterior circumstances of their lives, there are no essential differences between them and Therese Neumann. In each case it is the dolorous Way of the Cross which leads to the heights of Christian mysticism, in part even to its summit, the *unio mystica*, union with God. We see, too, that all cases of stigmatization (excepting, of course, any instances of fraud) arise exclusively from the fruitful soil of unadulterated Christianity, which is Catholicism. This soil, watered by participation in the spirit and the life of the Church through divine service and the Sacraments and conscientious fulfillment of all duties, and none other, can produce such flowers of mysticism. A predisposition thoroughly Catholic is essential. A vaguely, indefinable Christian attitude will not suffice. If the necessary qualifications exist, earnest personal cooperation will lead the soul upward until, having attained a measure of perfection, bestowal of the stigmata is possible. Stigmatization is not, however, universal or inevitable. When bestowed, it is a free gift of God, Who deigns to manifest Himself in this manner.

Of what does this predisposition consist; how does it develop itself? God sends suffering, which need not necessarily involve bodily disease. Nature resents this, rises in opposition, and man seeks by all the means at his disposal to free himself from pain. He asks God to lessen or to take away his suffering entirely. But he asks in vain. Then the soul comes to a fork in the road. It may choose to continue in impatient desire to be freed; and often there results a certain degree of resentment toward God. Or, realizing the will of God, the soul may submit to it and accept its suffering as a gift from Him Who chastises those whom He loves. This surrender to the will of God may advance by stages until it achieves an unconditional and joyous acceptance of present pain and also of whatever affliction may in the future be decreed for it. If the soul perseveres, if it passes successfully through the testing crucible of increased suffering, the reward is an intensified perception of divine things and a corresponding deepening of love for God. And the soul which suffers for love of God comes to an acute realization that, despite all His love for man, He is sinned against daily and hourly; and is led to offer itself in voluntary, vicarious atonement for these offenses. Then, by reason of its specific end, suffering attains a supernatural character, and in some instances a corresponding supernatural outward stamp, the stigmata. It is true, the marks of the Wounds are never bestowed upon one who is unworthy (though he who receives them may later prove himself unworthy), but they are not an essential of personal sanctity, for Heaven has many saints who were not stigmatized.

How does the Church test stigmatization? She declares that if the stigmata are the gifts of God, they who possess them will practice the Christian virtues with an ever-increasing ardor, not in single acts only but in all the affairs of life, so that their whole existence will be on a high plane. The words of Our Lord, "I confess to Thee, O Father, Lord of heaven and earth, because Thou hast hidden these things from the wise and prudent and hast revealed them to the little ones" (Luke 10:21) are applicable here. To call attention anew to the "way of spiritual childhood," and to teach us by her example how to walk in it, were the life tasks of the Little Flower. This is the way Therese Neumann has walked; to it the Voice directs her constantly. But scarcely one of the men of science, in attempting to explain the "phenomenon of Konnersreuth," has taken into account the predisposition of Therese Neumann, the atmosphere in which she has lived and the characteristics which found their fruition in the sacred marks which she bears. Science indeed!

UPHEAVAL OF THE COSMIC ORDER

Man, the lord of creation, deems himself the sovereign of the natural realm. A man of secular science declares that he "cannot believe in such an upheaval of the cosmic order" as the Konnersreuth phenomena involve. It irks man to be toppled from his throne, to be made to realize that he is not supreme. There must be a division of spirits, and if we wish to be understood by the general public, we must speak of things which are familiar to every poor Catholic servant-girl, but enigmas to the science of our godless age.

When we consider the charismata as supernatural gifts, we invade a field in which there is, to some extent, "an upheaval in the cosmic order." Men who have never lifted themselves above the sphere of natural living must look upon the supernatural as "an upheaval" and contrary to reason. In the natural order man is at the top; in the supernatural order at the bottom. In the former he is at the pinnacle of creation, in the latter God is all and man merely His creature, dependent upon Him for his very being. In the natural order we deal with the body, which is subject to natural laws; but in the supernatural order our concern is with the spirit, which is independent of natural laws. The soul which is still united with the body cannot by the use of its will power free itself from the natural law. But God can raise man, soul and body united, above the natural and place him in His realm of the supernatural. When this occurs, rapture, ecstasy, results; and according to the extent to which the border between nature and supernature is crossed, the natural laws, such as gravitation and sensory perception, cease to function. Body and soul remain united, though their separation may take place, temporarily. God is the absolute sovereign of this realm. He has not, however, shut Himself behind its portals, away from us. He has not made Himself inaccessible to man. He can be reached, most of all through prayer; and in the higher stages of the spiritual life, even mystical union with Him is possible.

The supernatural life is governed by laws, and the faithful observance of them enables us to determine with certainty whether fraud or self-deception prevails, or whether extraordinary things are genuinely supernatural. The basic law is this: God is the Creator, man the creature. God is all, and by His will He can cause man to be or cease to be. Man is as nothing. He cannot by exerting his will call himself into being. He exists only because God created him, poured a spirit into a material vessel. However exalted the position man may attain in the spiritual realm, he remains what he is essentially of himself—nothing.

Self-will, insistence upon gratification of one's own wishes, has no place in the supernatural sphere. When it invades this realm, it betrays the presence of deception, proves that the phenomena are not of God.

The prerequisite, then, of the first as of all subsequent steps in the spiritual life is the *de facto* acknowledgment of God. This acknowledgment must be an uninterrupted act. "My God and my all!," but I am nothing! This confession, developed until it has become a characteristic, a constant property of the soul, is called humility. It begins naturally with that which we describe as the submission of the human will to the Divine Will; that is, with the expression through deeds of the aforementioned relationship between God and man. In the natural realm the will is paramount. Man's freedom of the will is respected by God Himself. The will causes us to decide for good or evil; it determines our attitude toward God. Man is free to misuse his will, and it is misused whenever it is directed against the known will of God. And man is so absolutely the master of his will that he can surrender it, but he ought to do this only when he has the assurance that this surrender will not involve him in opposition to the Lord. Such an assurance is impossible when the subjection is solely to another human will; but it is present when the subjection is to the will of God, for God wills nothing in opposition to Himself.

Humility, submission to the Divine Will, issues in action, and this is obedience. Humility in action means obedience to the will of God, which is made manifest, above all, in the Ten Commandments, and in the Great Law of the New Testament, the precept of love of one's neighbor, be he friend or enemy. When a soul has been distinguished by extraordinary gifts, so that it is lifted above the natural order of things, we can ascertain by the soul's attitude whether its gifts are of God. Does it observe all the Commandments faithfully? Does it love its neighbor, and its enemy? If it does not, there is opposition to the will of God on the part of this soul and the extraordinary things it possesses are not of God.

Prudence is the correct use of reason. This virtue entails the subjection of man's passions to the restrictions imposed by God's laws. If the intellect is misused, if it is permitted to be dominated by man's lower nature, there is self-will. And the presence of self-will in the spiritual life may show itself in visions and revelations, prophecies, etc. It induces disregard of the authority with which Christ invested His Church, and when this takes place, there is danger of fraud or self-deception, or that the phenomena are of a demoniacal origin.

Submission to the will of God means to wait until God speaks or acts, and this waiting upon Him is called patience. When it is wanting, there is no genuine subjection to the Divine Will, no sincere acknowledgment of His right to have His will prevail.

Another touchstone of the highest value is faith, an unconditional acceptance of all which God has revealed because He has revealed it. Faith involves a new concept, that of the Church. By what means is the true revelation transmitted to us and its authenticity guaranteed and safeguarded? By what means can we ascertain with the assurance of faith, whether or not a revelation is divine? The Old Testament possessed, in addition to God's personal guidance, its authoritative teachers and its prophetical books. But the New Testament has Christ and His work, the Church which He established with Himself as the head and the Pope His vicar on earth. That He would be with His Church to the end of time is the promise of the Divine Founder, and where Christ, where God is, error cannot abide, nor anything contrary to the Eternal Truth; that is, to God Himself.

As to what the Catholic deposit of faith contains, there can be no doubt. One might ask this question concerning the many religious organizations of human origin, but one must admit that the Catholic Church has always striven to define each truth so precisely that all men can understand what it means. The teaching of the Church adheres scrupulously to the word and to the spirit of Christ, which are her absolute governing norms. But that the will of man interprets variously the meaning of Christ's words, is proved by the multiplicity of sects, all of which assert that they are based on His utterances. Who shall answer Pilate's question, "What is truth?" Who dares to answer it? No human authority, but a divine one only can give a reply consonant with the truth. The Catholic Church is the only church which maintains that she has divine authority. And she proves her right to this distinction. How jealously she guards her patrimony of the faith, not, however, as a buried treasure, but as something which lives and increases, a vital organism which grows and develops and evolves.

Since the doctrines of the Catholic Church are divinely revealed, divinely set forth, it is the duty of man to accept them, to believe in them. Any man who would raise himself and his life above the natural into the supernatural spiritual life, must accordingly maintain complete agreement with the Catholic faith, even in the natural order. Submission to the teaching of the Church and a mode of life consonant therewith, which entails unconditional obedience to her authority and observance of her regulations as to faith and morals, are further essential prerequisites of harmony in the supernatural sphere. For the authority of the Church is none other than the authority of Christ Himself, Whose heir the Church is. In the natural life of man obedience to the legitimate bearer of ecclesiastical authority plays an immensely important, a decisive part. Authority combined with right constitutes a basic means of distinguishing between the supernaturally true and false. Rightful authority is by nature a possession of parents. According to the law of Christ, it is hierarchically possessed by the parish priest, the bishop, the Pope as representing Christ. By their mouths God speaks in matters of the soul, in its relation to God. *(Religio* means a binding.) To deny obedience to this authority is to place oneself in opposition to God, and this is the second reason why obedience is such an important touchstone.

What we have said provides a test adequate for a private verdict.

We have considered the chief principles according to

which the Church judges. For the present, the only judgment within the province of her authority is to decide whether or not there is present anything contrary to the Catholic faith or contrary to Christian morals. But she has thus far had no occasion to make any remonstrance in the case of Therese Neumann, and has therefore permitted her representative, Father Naber, to continue in his position. She has advised care and prudence. She has supported Father Naber. And he, judging her in the light of the principles enumerated, has stretched his paternal hand protectingly over Therese, and to all who ask him he answers unhesitatingly that he believes in the supernatural origin of her stigmata. For a score of years he has been Therese's parish priest and spiritual director; he knows her thoroughly by virtue of daily observance. He is aware of her humility and patience, her meekness; her love for parents and brothers and sisters and her neighbor; her love of God, her faith, her prudence, and especially her obedience in the most varied circumstances. His conclusion is based upon long and immediate experience combined with a thorough theological training, and surely it bears far more weight than the verdicts dependent upon a few days' merely external observation on the part of those who deem themselves experts. The deceased Dr. A. von Henle, Bishop of Regensburg, who had not himself seen Therese Neumann, declared that "Resl is a good child." How she measures up to this estimate the reader can judge for himself. We shall continue to give ample material upon which to base a verdict.

Let us, in concluding this section of our book, consider some of the objections which have been made against acceptance of the stigmata as of supernatural origin.

As has been said, stigmatization's outward expression is manifold. The wounds may be invisible and perceptible to the sufferer only because of the pain they cause, as in the case of Sister Mary Fidelis Weiss. They may be visible only at specific intervals, as with Gemma Galgani, whose stigmata could be seen on Fridays throughout two years and then became invisible until her death. Again, as the history of Anna Catherine Emmerick shows, the wounds may remain visible until the end of life. Some of the stigmata bleed, some do not. Some of them retain the character of open wounds. In the case of Sister Mary of Jesus Crucified, they were like nailheads in the palms. The wound of the heart may be on the right side, as it was on the Body of Christ, or on the left side, or directly above the heart itself. Of many stigmatists, Sister Mary Frances of the Five Wounds of Christ, the Neapolitan nun who was canonized in 1867, might serve best as a prototype of Therese Neumann; though, as I have said, no two instances of stigmatization exactly alike are known to me. Sister Mary Frances was twenty-eight years of age when she received the marks of the Wounds, she bore them for twenty-seven years, during the last of which they were invisible but the pain caused by them the more intense. They opened only after the Vespers of Thursday during the month of March. After the hour of Christ's death on Fridays a thin membrane covered them, but they remained visible. If one were to make a demand which is theologically untenable—and it has been made—that the stigmata agree absolutely in all respects with the Wounds of the Saviour, one would betray a crass misconception of their significance. It would amount almost to dictation to God as to how He shall bestow His gifts of grace so that man will deign to acknowledge them.

It has been asserted that the stigmata, in order to be genuine and of supernatural origin, must not appear until the one who receives them has reached the highest stage of mysticism; and that the mystic thus distinguished must be permeated by a sense of supreme joy. The facts of experience do not bear out these contentions. In most instances, the bestowal of the stigmata is coincident with an increase of suffering, and the summit of the mystic ascent is still far distant. If God gives His gifts and wishes them to remain hidden, He chooses cloistered souls to receive them. If He wishes His gifts to become known, "that the world may know that there is a Higher Power"; if He wishes to increase the faith of those in the world, for whom also He died, then He selects the marketplace of the world and works His miracles upon one in the midst of the world, such as Therese Neumann. It is a severe test of her humility, but out of obedience she submitted, though she was aware that opprobrium would be heaped upon her. She endures this suffering, too, in the spirit of the Redeemer: *propter nos homines et propter nostram salutem.*

Are the stigmata the effects of an abnormal imagination produced by the reading of mystical books? As Father Naber has said, Therese has never read books of this kind. Neither did any of the stigmatists whose biographies are known to us. Their mysticism grew directly out of their lives; it was not studied. It was a mysticism of living and suffering. We know of many readers of mystical literature—Sister Mary Fidelis Weiss warns against them—but though humanly speaking they might appear to possess the prerequisites to a greater extent, stigmatization is not vouchsafed to them. Every director of souls will substantiate this assertion.[52]

In the life's story of Sister Mary of Jesus Crucified we read how she, like Therese Neumann, did not comprehend what had happened when she received the marks of the Wounds. No one explained the matter to her and for years she was under the impression that she was a leper. She concentrated all the force of her will upon effecting their removal, because she feared that her bleeding wounds would cause her to be a burden to her sisters in religion. She used all available means in the hope of curing the "disease." On May 6, 1867, her mistress of novices at the Carmel of Pau commanded her to ask God to withdraw the stigmata. Sister Mary obeyed this command, and at the intercession of Our Lady her petition was granted at the beginning of the next Lent. The marks disappeared for nine months. In 1876, when the superior at the Carmel of Bethlehem explained the meaning of the "disease" to her, Sister Mary in an ecstasy begged God to remove the visible marks, "if it is not contrary to Thy will." She received this answer: "The roses are for others, the thorns (suffering) are for you."[53]

THE SIXTH AND SEVENTH CURES

On February 13, 1926, the suffering which preceded the bestowal of the stigmata had begun, and Therese was again forced to take to her bed, which she was not able to leave until May 17 of that year.

On this latter day, after the midday meal, just as Father Naber had entered the room, in the midst of a conversation, the sentence she was speaking left half unfinished, she was rapt in ecstasy, the Light shone once more and the familiar Voice spoke to her: "Be patient and do not become discouraged! Today you shall experience a little alleviation. But you shall have much to suffer. I have helped you hitherto and have always told you that you need not fear. Stay humble and do not lose your childlike spirit."

Therese did not believe that the alleviation had already begun. She experienced no change and when her mother rearranged the bed, the daughter could not stand, her knees trembled and refused to support her. This was told to Father Naber, who thereupon left the Neumann house. A short time afterwards there was a knock at his door, and Therese stood before him. After his departure she had, though still without expectation, endeavored to walk, and found that she could do so. From the bed of sickness she had walked, alone, to the church to thank God. From the church she had gone to the rectory.

The anniversary of the Little Flower's death, September 30, 1926, was not an uneventful day. The Light and the Voice came once more, but we know only that Therese was informed that she would still have much to endure.

Meanwhile, the Friday visions and ecstasies continued. Therese saw the Passion from the Agony in the Garden to the Death on the Cross. She witnessed the suffering of the Redeemer and shared in it. Her participation in the Passion involved physical pain. On November 19, her suffering with the Saviour was so intense, its effect so extraordinarily vehement that towards six o'clock in the evening one expected her death momentarily. On the Feast of the Sacred Heart of the year 1926, the first Friday of June, the wounds of the crown of thorns were bestowed upon Therese, and though they were then invisible and remained so for some time, their coming was accompanied by additional, lasting pain. She said nothing except to observe that now there was scarcely a spot on her body that did not cause her pain, and no one knew what had happened. Early on the morning of the November 19 mentioned above, Therese seemed to be dying and Extreme Unction was administered. But during the forenoon, while she was in ecstasy, blood poured suddenly out of the eight wounds of the head, and as the white head-covering betrayed the blood, the secret was revealed. Since then these wounds have bled during each of the Friday agonies. In the afternoon a true death struggle took place at the conclusion of the Passion experience, and severe choking spells caused those about her to fear that the end was near. Her condition was due in part to pneumonia and bronchitis, from both of which she had suffered for some time, and both of which were now in an acutely grave stage. As the hour of six in the evening approached, she lay ashen pale and dissolution seemed at hand. The death candle was given to her and she grasped it. In the other hand she held the death crucifix, and Father Naber and his curate recited the prayers with which the Church accompanies the departing souls of her children.

Very suddenly Therese loosened her hold on the candle, the crucifix was let fall, and with one violent motion she sat up. A happy smile transformed her face and as in her ecstasies, she raised her arms toward an object which only she could see. Suddenly her breathing was normal, and those about her bed, still under the spell of the preceding hours, could not immediately realize what had occurred. From out of the Light the Voice had spoken, and awkwardly, striving to find the correct manner in which to relate her experience, Therese told what had been announced to her: "Your complete submission is a cause of joy to the Saviour. You shall not die now. What has happened had this purpose, to show the world that there is a Higher Power. You shall continue to suffer, and in that way cooperate with the priests in saving souls."

The next day she was about as usual.

One cannot maintain that this was the natural course of the two diseases which had brought Therese to the threshold of death. And whosoever sees self-deception in the accompanying Light and Voice cannot demand credence for his assertion until he produces irrefutable proof. Assertions are not proofs. Therese's conscientiousness and truthfulness, which none impugns, make it impossible not to believe her words. The death-agony and the sudden cure are facts to which those present, all of them honorable people, are ready to testify. Father Naber, during his many years of pastoral work, had often ministered at the bedside of the dying; his was the trained observation of long experience. The world had in very truth been shown "that there is a Higher Power," and that it is master of life and death.

CHAPTER V
THE SEERESS OF KONNERSREUTH

THE CHRISTMAS VISION

N Christmas Eve of the year 1926, a Friday, Therese lay exhausted in her bed after the poignant experience of the regular Friday ecstasy. The members of the family had gone to Midnight Mass; all excepting her father, who remained at home to watch at his daughter's bedside. He sat and read to her Goffine's explanation of the Christmas Gospel. From the steeple of the village church near by came the tolling of the bells to mark the climax of the Holy Sacrifice of the Mass, the solemn moment of consecration. Herr Neumann knelt in adoration. He was aroused from his pious thoughts by an exclamation from the smiling lips of his daughter. He saw her hearken, as to something as yet far away but drawing nearer. Her eyes were large and bright with expectation, and she sat up in her bed. Her rapturous vision lasted a long time, and when the Midnight Mass was ended and the mother and brothers and sisters returned home, one of the latter hurried to call Father Naber. Suddenly Therese sank back in the pillow ... the vision had left. Softly she said, as if to herself: "Now I would be glad to die. ... It is always beautiful there. I should like to go, I should like to die. It is so dull here." After several attempts Father Naber succeeded in establishing the sequence of mental impressions by using the phrase, "The Christ Child has come!" Therese's thoughts clarified at the sound of these words, and she spoke, joyously: "Ah, yes, it was the

Christ Child!" She had been awakened by wondrously sweet song and music. Then the familiar Light appeared and the Voice she had heard so often: "You are permitted not only to suffer with the dear Saviour, you shall be joyful with Him, too. But remain submissive and childlike." Then she raised herself up, and suddenly all about her there was another incomparably brighter light. "And I saw a little child above me, on a cloud as it were. Oh, it was so beautiful! And I saw the child in the midst of the light. It had the most tender, rosy cheeks, not deeply red, but just a little, and the dearest of little feet! ... The soft hair was blond and framed the smiling face in golden curls. With bright, deep-blue eyes it looked at me so mildly. The child wore a little dress. It stretched its arms out to me and smiled at me. It was as though the child wished to come to me!"

Therese had been deeply impressed by the song which she heard while rapt in the vision, but at the time she could not grasp its meaning. Professor Wutz of Eichstätt, who visited her soon afterwards, solved the problem. He repeated the words of the angel, "Glory to God in the highest ..." in a number of languages, but each time Therese shook her head, saying, "No, that is not what it said." As if doing so casually, he uttered the Aramaic words, and Therese interrupted him, joyously. "That is it! That is what the song said! But there is still a little missing."

Since this night Therese ceased to take even liquid food. Father Naber tried repeatedly to induce her to drink a little tea or raspberry juice, but he was compelled to admit again and again that her stomach could not receive even the smallest amount.

Imagination? What one imagines is in the consciousness and its meaning is known. One does not require the aid of another to clarify what one has imagined, particularly when the meaning lies so close at hand. And can one imagine Aramaic words which one has never heard; imagine them in such a way that one recognizes them at once and distinguishes them from other words no less foreign? Was not Aramaic the vernacular of Palestine when Christ was born? I will content myself with putting the question.

THERESE NEUMANN IN ECSTASY

The visions, which began with that of the Passion during the Holy Week of 1926, and which have continued regularly since then (excepting only for interruptions based on the liturgy) are in the case of Therese Neumann combined with the ecstatic state. The ecstasy begins with the condition familiar to mysticism, the *raptus,* an immediate and instantaneous enrapture which is united with the vision. Once, in the midst of her description of her pet goldfinch, she was abruptly transported into the state of ecstasy. "Often in the middle of a word, in the midst of activities which carry Therese's thoughts far from spiritual things," writes Baron Aretin, "the ecstasies break upon her like the storm of a primeval world. They tear her from the pillow into postures which are often, physically speaking, violations of the law of gravitation; and draw her arms forward and upward. Only the play of her features, now animated and readable beyond all precedent, shows what she is undergoing."[54]

"Frequently, on Thursday evenings, the parish priest endeavored by all available means to divert the invalid and to forestall even the possibility that suggestion might play a part in producing the ecstasy. But his efforts were always futile."[55] During one of the pauses of from ten to fifteen minutes, by which the ecstasies of the Passion are invariably interrupted, Therese receives Holy Communion. "The acolyte, who carries the lantern and the priest's surplice back to the church, has scarcely descended the stairs, when the stigmatist is hurled from her pillow. Half lying, half sitting, at an acute angle, in a position which would normally be found extremely tiring and well-nigh impossible, she stretches out her arms. They are steady, as though supported somehow in the air. The fingers, especially the thumbs, are turned slightly inward. The stigmata glow with ruby freshness. At intervals, the arms move back and forth, almost imperceptibly. The face, framed by the white head-cloth and streaked with the streams of blood from the eyes, is raised up and its posture is like that of a blind man who is listening intently, who has no earthly orientation, and who lives and sees only in his soul."[56]

"During each of the separate ecstasies Therese is wholly indifferent to, nay beyond the reach of outward influences. She replies to no questions, responds to no shaking of the hand. A fly which alighted on the closed eye and which was purposely not shooed away, remained on the same spot for five minutes and Therese gave no evidence of being in the least annoyed by it. In the square below, the funeral procession of an old soldier passes by, with the blare and blast of martial music by the veterans' band from Waldsassen. The windows rattle, but the ecstatic does not move in the least. Awakening and falling back upon the pillow, she answers questions. But her consciousness is limited to what she has just seen. She is totally ignorant of what is still to come. And the remembrance of the affairs of ordinary life is extinguished. It is noteworthy that, in the middle of a sentence of her answer, Therese will again be rapt into ecstasy."[57]

The separate ecstasies during the visions of the Passion last no more than five, ten, or twelve minutes, but that of the Crucifixion uninterruptedly for one hour and a quarter (at least on the day I was present). "I employed the pauses between the ecstasies," writes Dr. Hollnsteiner, "in gaining information as to the content of her visions. Father Naber aided me in the most generous manner, asking Therese the questions I wished to have her answer. It became apparent that she has a very clear picture of Christ and of all He does and suffers. But for the physical world she exhibits but little interest. It is, in her estimation, of no importance. ... What she sees in her ecstasies is remembered with the utmost clearness. In this regard, the following impressed me as highly significant: After she had seen the Saviour carry His Cross and fall beneath it the first time, Father Naber at my request tried to lead her to a consideration of the Crucifixion. All his efforts failed. She maintained stoutly that 'the dear Saviour would not be nailed to the Cross.' But when this last and most terrible scene of the Passion had been witnessed by her, she described with the minutest details the climax of Our Redeemer's sufferings and the most awful event in history. However, of the personages concerned, she recognizes only Christ and His Mother. ..."[58]

Another writes of a joyful ecstasy of Therese's which he witnessed: "Her countenance was as if transfigured. She stretched out her hands, farther and farther, as though she wished to embrace what she saw. Did she not, perhaps, see the Annunciation, since on this day the Church celebrates that mystery? (Such was, in fact, the case.—*Author.*) This condition of unearthly, blessed joy lasted some seven or eight minutes, an incomparable, heart-touching contrast to the preceding spectacle of agony. Then she sank back upon the bed. A look of wistful disappointment swept across her face. The glory and beauty have vanished; heavenly things have been withdrawn."[59]

A semiecstatic state is wont to succeed Therese's ecstasies. She is no longer the enraptured seeress, but she describes what has been impressed upon her with extraordinary sharpness, and replies to inquiries, though she is still wrapt up in what she has seen and still is actively participating in it. The condition is a more than natural one, because, as I was able to establish, while it lasts she possesses the power of hierognosis, the discernment of relics.

During the semiecstatic periods Therese's mental conceptions are those of a child, and her manner of expression conforms to them. To be present during these conversations of a soul of childlike piety with its God are among the most touching and beautiful experiences I have had, and I shall dwell upon them later. The ecstatic is unable to comprehend such simple concepts as brother, sister, parents, and numbers. In describing the discovery of the True Cross, she declared that the Cross of the Saviour consisted (since the longer section had been cut into two) of four parts. She said, one and one and one and one. "That is four?" asked Father Naber. "Four? I do not know. There was one and one and one and one." The cross of the penitent thief consisted of three parts. "Three? I do not know. One and one and one." Questioned about the illumination in the Garden of Olives, she related, says Baron Aretin, a witness, that "there was a big light, and then there was a fire of logwood and another fire of logwood." She uses the purest Upper Palatinate dialect and her expressions are of the most primitive sort imaginable. For instance, in order to express the concept of Pope, she spoke of "him who comes after the one who cut off the ear"; in another case, "he who came after the one at whom the cock crew so." Thus in two scenes the figure of Peter played the chief roles, and they were especially vivid in her memory because in each of them the action was directed against the Redeemer. That Peter presumed to cut off the ear of Malchus is vehemently resented by Therese, because one dared to "carry on so" in the presence of Our Lord. In her semiecstatic state Saint Peter is invariably referred to by her as "the one who cut off the ear." Saint John is called "the young man"; Pilate "has no hair on his head and around his mouth"; Caiphas is the man "with the mocking lips and the big white beard"; the penitent thief is "the good man," and the other thief "the bad man." Baron Aretin says: "Having forgotten completely all that had been learned—I repeat that I report only what I have personally observed—her sympathies are extended to Pilate, who treated Our Lord with consideration; and even to Judas who gave Him a kiss. She does not, of course, understand the Aramaic cry of the disciples, Galapa! Galapa! (Traitor! Traitor!), and betrayal is not a visually representable object, or was not, in this instance at least, so represented. She disapproves of Peter, whose sword-thrust caused the first blood to flow. And when my guide (Professor Wutz) interposed, 'Why, Resl, today you seem to be a bit stupid,' she retorted quickly, 'And I believe you are even more stupid!'

"Her utter ignorance of what is to come is remarkable. After each succeeding separate ecstasy, which at first last only a few minutes each, she is convinced that Our Lord is to be set free, and she does not understand at all when my guide tells her what must follow. She is under the impression that Professor Wutz (who hears what she says during the ecstasies) stands back of her, and that therefore she cannot see him during the vision. She said to him, when the cross-bearing Saviour had reached the outskirts of the city, 'Hurry, now, to His Mother and tell her that they have set Him free!' She insists upon this even after she has been told by Professor Wutz that he has been told how the people have planned to kill Jesus, and finally she compromises by saying, 'Well, tell her (the Mother of Christ) that Resl says they will set Him free.' When the place of execution is reached, she reassures herself with the words, 'They forced Him to carry timbers to this place.' Let it be said in explanation that in her visions, the Redeemer does not carry a cross but three separate beams, which are not joined until Golgatha is reached and are then made to form a large Y."[60]

The same matter is described by another witness, the Reverend Father Schilcher of Hasberg, in October, 1927: "Following another vision, she lies, smiling joyfully, and then Professor Wutz, who knows the content of the vision, asks her whether the Jews have removed the three beams from the Redeemer's shoulders. His voice is so low that I can scarcely hear it. I draw closer and I hear her answer: 'Yes; and now He can go home!' 'Oh, no!' objects the professor, 'now He is going to be nailed to the Cross!' ... 'No, no, He can go home!' ... 'But, Resl, you know that He must die!' ... 'No, He can go home!' "[61]

All who have listened for hours, as I have, to conversations such as these, will agree that Therese's childlike condition is not self-induced, or feigned. It seems to be a charismatic gift accompanying the ecstasy, and perhaps it is based on the fact that, by emptying the memory of all else, it prevents anything learned at school or later, from being added to the vision content. Therese is probably intended to be a connecting link between the actualities, sensibly seen by her, of nearly two thousand years ago and us, who live in the twentieth century after Christ's birth. Again we are reminded of Our Lord's expression of thanks to His Heavenly Father for having revealed to the children and the simple what He hides from the wise ones of the world. And perhaps this childlike condition is a part of the "little way" which Therese Neumann has selected to walk in imitation of Saint Thérèse of the Infant Jesus, the way of spiritual childhood. Neither is this a novelty in the Catholic Church. Many have preceded our two Thereses in this path. Of the stigmatist to whom we have previously referred, Saint Mary Frances of the Five Wounds of Christ (1715-1791), her biographer has said: "She practiced the highest and most characteristic devotion to the sacred childhood of Jesus, the one most pleasing to Our Lord and most advantageous to our Saint, by preserving so faithfully the spirit of the divine childhood, the innocence and simplicity, the submissiveness and unaffected ardor of a holy child, and taking it undiminished and unalloyed with her to her grave."[62]

Little Saint Thérèse spoke these prophetic words on her deathbed: "I feel that my mission is soon to begin—my mission to make others love God as I love Him ... to teach souls my 'little way' ... I will spend my heaven in doing good upon earth." She would, solely out of love, return to the earth, so that the Eternal Love might be loved. "It (the 'little way') is the way of spiritual childhood, the way of trust and absolute self-surrender."[63]

Therese Neumann learned of this way many years ago. It was pointed out to her by my guide, in Konnersreuth, whom she calls "Uncle"; she has traveled it with unswerving fidelity, and to this she owes, no doubt, the spiritual roses which the Little Flower has showered down upon her.

Verily, these are things which have been hidden from the worldly wise, for many of those who have written of the "riddle of Konnersreuth" have failed to make use of this essential key to the understanding of Therese Neumann's soul. They dip their pens awkwardly in the ink of the material, and because they lack a supernatural faith, many things which they see are inexplicable to them. It is futile to speak to a blind man of the colors of the rainbow, of all the beauties of God's creation.

OTHER VISIONS

In addition to the regularly recurring Friday visions, Therese Neumann has been granted other visions, among them that of Christmas, which has been described.

"On March 25, 1927, the Feast of the Annunciation, which fell on a Friday, she had as usual endured her excruciating participation in the Passion, and lay on her pillow as if dead. The stillness of death prevails in the room. Not the slightest breath, not the least movement evidences life. Is she really dead? After considerable time her spiritual director speaks to her. Gradually she regains consciousness. But there ensues a martyrdom, a terrifying combat with phlegm, a life-and-death struggle for breath. She had already the day before suffered intensely on this account. Not until she had wrestled desperately for almost half an hour did relief come from phlegm. And then she sank back into her pillow, utterly exhausted. ... I am about to leave, after having stood perseveringly in the same place for two hours. ... Nor was I to regret my vigil. For suddenly Therese jerks herself up from the pillow. Is there to be another vomiting spell? No, no! See, what a spectacle! A second ecstasy has been vouchsafed to the sufferer! Her countenance beams with supernal joy. She stretches out her arms, farther and farther, as though they must at all costs embrace what she sees." (Pfarrer C. Vogl.)

It had, indeed, been a vision of the Annunciation, as Father Naber and Professor Wutz managed to establish by questioning the seeress. A poor, pictureless room of one window only, and a bare earthen floor. A young maiden kneeling on a bolster, her arms crossed over her breast, absorbed in a manuscript roll (the Sacred Scriptures). Of a sudden an angel appears, of so great a brightness that words cannot describe it. But Therese can gaze upon the brightness in spite of its intensity. The two speak to each other, but Therese can understand nothing. The maiden does not use many words in answering. The angel, however, speaks much more. When she addresses the angel, the maiden spreads out her hands (the Jewish gesture of prayer!). Her garment is blue, but not sky-blue. At the middle it is drawn together by a girdle. Father Naber suggested to Therese that surely she must know the maiden. No, she does not. But it seems to her that the maiden looked like the Mother of God (as seen by Therese at the foot of the cross), but very much younger.

Professor Wutz spoke a few sentences in foreign tongues, asking Therese whether the angel's words sounded like them. Repeatedly she gave a negative answer, and declared that his words were totally unknown to her. Again Dr. Wutz speaks a sentence, and Therese beams with glad surprise. "Yes, yes, that is what he said! But something is missing." The seeress has struck it right again. The last words used by Professor Wutz were

Aramaic, the language of Palestine in the days of Christ's earthly sojourn. This discernment of languages is a testimony of great weight in favor of the genuineness of her ecstasies. Deception and fraud would entangle themselves hopelessly.

"Was it not remarkable, too, that the three birds in the room, hitherto so quiet that we were unaware of their presence, began to sing during the second ecstasy, and sang so jubilantly, with such exuberance that one could scarcely hear another's voice and we were obliged to quiet them, again and again, each time in vain, of course."[64]

On August 6, 1926, Therese saw in ecstatic vision the Transfiguration of Our Lord on Mount Tabor. On the same Feast of the following year this vision was repeated. This is Herr Angerer's description of the one of 1926:

"It was the hour of sunset. The mount was flat, unlike Calvary. But it, too, was rocky. The Saviour wore His reddish-brown robe and across His shoulder a cloth like a mantle. He prayed, standing. Three lay there and slept. ... Suddenly Our Lord raised Himself about half a meter from the earth. The whole garment became white, a peculiar whiteness. The best comparison I know is snow-white. His countenance was luminous ... but the light of His face was not blinding. I saw His eyes and His entire face. Under His feet there was a thick cloud. Our Lord looked upwards, in the midst of all at me once, then upwards again. At His right side a man with a splendid long beard stood on another cloud. His garment had many folds, it was almost like a mantle. At His left side there stood a man whose beard was not so long. His garment was girdled and he had a mantle, too. The two on either side of the Redeemer spoke with Him.

"All at once the three below awoke from their sleep and said something, especially the one who had previously sat to the right of Jesus. He had short hair and was apparently the oldest of the three. To the left sat the one who stands under the cross. He had no beard. Toward the front sat one who was older than the one I believe was John. Suddenly it seemed as though the three were filled with fear. They fell forward upon their faces. There was a great cloud and I saw no more of the three above. Then there was a voice, a clear, strong voice, but I did not understand what it said. And then Our Lord stood there again as before, and He went to the three who had been with Him from the beginning and took the one on the right by his right arm. The Saviour said something to him ... and all disappeared! The light in the midst of which I saw the Saviour during His Transfiguration was far brighter and more glorious and beautiful than the light which I saw in the other visions. Compared with the light of the Transfiguration, that of the other visions is like the pale light of the stars."[65]

On Holy Thursday of 1927, Therese saw the Last Supper and the institution of the Holy Eucharist. "Another detail which testifies to Therese's faculty of observation was given me (by Dr. Wutz) writes Baron von Aretin. "At the Last Supper she was amazed at the attitude of the Apostles. It was by no means devout, and it betrayed an utter lack of understanding. Of one of the Twelve she declared bluntly that he looked frightfully stupid. 'But, Resl, you ought not to say that. He was a good man.' ... 'Have you never seen a good man who looks stupid?' According to the Bible, the Apostles contended on this occasion, in spite of the atmosphere of the Passion already enveloping them, as to which was the greatest among them.

"I was privileged to take part in the official recording of the vision of Pentecost Monday, in which Peter returned to the Upper Room and repeated the breaking and distribution of the bread. And there came again the sound as of a mighty wind (the descent of the Holy Ghost) which had been part of the vision on Pentecost itself. But this time the mien of the Apostles was exceedingly earnest and collected. I cannot imagine a more effective presentation of the miraculous change which Pentecost wrought in the Apostles.

"The reproduction of the Aramaic words on the part of Therese in normal state is, despite its imperfections, so exact that Dr. Wutz is able to distinguish the Galilean dialect of Peter from the purer Judean speech of Caiphas. I was witness of this when, on July 11 of this year (1927), we recorded after a lapse of five weeks, what Therese had seen from the night of Pentecost Sunday to the morning of the next day. I should like to use as an example the speech of Peter's before the Sanhedrin on the morning of Pentecost Monday. Therese related: 'When he began to speak, Peter pointed to the man beside him, who had been healed. Then he drew his right hand through his hair and finally he pointed vehemently with his right hand to the high priests seated before him, and said (there followed some ten Aramaic words). And the conclusion of his speech was: (again a number of Aramaic words).' The words of Peter when he pointed to his judges were, in English: 'By the name of Our Lord Jesus Christ of Nazareth, Whom you crucified!' (Acts 4:10.) And those of his conclusion were in reference to the stone which was rejected by the builders. So Therese had heard perfectly, though she could not understand them, the words which synchronized with the Apostle's gestures. Peter and John were released by Caiphas and together with the man who had been healed, they left the court. 'As they go out, Calvary is to the right, immediately in front of me the temple,' is Therese's report. I notice that Dr. Wutz is astounded. It developed that, upon leaving Caiphas's court, the two Apostles on their return to the room of the Last Supper, selected a gate which forced them to make a little detour."[66]

On the morning of Easter Sunday, 1927, Therese's vision was of the Saviour's Resurrection and the coming of the four women to the tomb. She saw how Mary Magdalen alone entered the tomb and then, terrified, found Our Lord in the garden; how the risen Christ looked upon her with infinite love and held His pierced Hands out toward her.[67]

Of two other visions, the martyrdom of Saint Lawrence, patron of the Konnersreuth parish church on August 10, 1927, and on August 15, 1927, that of the death and assumption into heaven of the Mother of God, we have, unfortunately, no detailed accounts from trustworthy sources. Therese saw the martyrdom of Saint Lawrence on August 10, which is the liturgical feast-day of this Saint, though it is celebrated the Sunday following. I know that on the day of the first of these visions, Father Naber read the Laurentian antiphons to Therese with the words spoken by him, whereupon she affirmed that they agreed with the words heard during the vision.

As the Church has not spoken in regard to these visions, has not declared that they do not contain anything contrary to the Catholic faith and the Sacred Scriptures, nor that they may be considered as emanating from supernatural illumination, they possess no more than the character of private expressions on the part of Therese Neumann. As such they have been dealt with, and reference to the sources have been duly noted; and the same applies to the Friday vision, in regard to which I shall relate my personal experience.

MY VISIT TO KONNERSREUTH

Autumn comes early up there in the pine-covered highlands. Mists hung about us as we journeyed from Waldsassen toward Konnersreuth on the afternoon of Thursday, August 25, 1927. As we neared the village, which is in a valley and surmounted by trees, I could not repress a feeling of uneasiness, for it seemed to me not that I was to look upon Therese Neumann, but that she was to look upon me. My companion was an aged priest, a domestic prelate of His Holiness the Pope, the head of an important cathedral chapter, who had been for many years associated as vicar-general with one of the most eminent Princes of the Church in our days. He had been for a long period the spiritual director of Barbara Pfister, the stigmatized virgin of Speyer, who died in 1909, and possesses exceptional experience in the evaluation of extraordinary psychic phenomena. When we reached the village at four o'clock, we were met by Herr D. W. Mut, as had been prearranged. Of his acquaintanceship with Therese Neumann, something has already been said. In such company, I was assured of the most gracious reception and most generous accommodations.

Konnersreuth has in its center the massive village church, around which the houses are grouped. Beside the church is the school, and directly back of it, the home of the parish priest, on a knoll and with a flight of stone steps leading to the door. From our quarters we strolled across the square, past the house of Therese's parents, an humble one-story home, in the attic of which a little room has been built in for the stigmatist. The house had not been large enough, and the influx of visitors made repairs urgent, so

Mr. Neumann enlarged and improved it a bit, with funds borrowed from his sister, a credit union, and the parish. But the sum was not sufficient, so all the members of the family, including Therese, took part in the building work. The scaffolds are still standing, the wall-finish is still fresh, and the smell of lime fills the air, so Therese has since two weeks ago been partaking of the rectory's hospitality and occupies the first-floor room in which the parish priest ordinarily received his callers.

A small swarm of people at the door of the rectory tells us where to find Therese. The village has already received many visitors, in expectation of the next day, Friday. Quietly, absorbed, the people move about, none concerning himself with the others, because each one is even now concerned solely with the stigmatist. Scarcely have we reached the rectory when we see Father Naber coming toward us, and immediately upon the exchange of greetings and introductions we are ushered into the house. We speak a few words in the hall, then Father Naber opens the first door to the left and we enter. Against the left wall, between two windows with flowers, there is a sofa and on it sits Therese Neumann behind a large tapestry-covered table. She is speaking with a number of persons standing near her. Then she sees us, smiles, and a look of inquiry united with retiring modesty in her tender, light-blue eyes is our greeting. Her face has a healthy color. It is framed in a white head-cloth, the two ends of which hang forward over her shoulders. The neat, slender figure is clothed in a simple black dress; and her hands, to which I direct my gaze, are covered by black half-gloves, or mitts. On the table in front of her are flowers which have been given to her, a number of letters and pictures. Father Naber makes the brief presentations, produces chairs, and we seat ourselves. Pointing to the pictures, I ask her whether she would accept a picture of the Sacred Heart which I have brought along for her, and she accepts it with thanks. "Uncle" Mut, who is seated next to her, is at once drawn into conversation with her, to whom he is friend and confidant, and I have ample opportunity to study Therese Neumann.

The stigmatist's speech, in which the dialect of the Upper Palatinate is now slightly discernible, is natural, of artless modesty, and engaging simplicity. There is nothing artificial, nothing affected about her. Her views are thoroughly sound and all her interests have as their ultimate object the Saviour Whom she loves so much. Though her countenance is pale, one cannot say that she looks unhealthy. It is evident that she has no desire to appear exceptional, or to be unusual. Her clear blue eyes bespeak the peace of her soul; they are merry, not moody or melancholy. Her whole personality is one of complete self-possession, and I can thoroughly understand Father Naber's statement: "Therese is a simple, natural child, the simplest child in the parish." All that happens about her and through her seems to her something matter-of-course; and in view of her spiritual experiences, she probably has no reason to be easily stirred to wonder.

The conversation developed into such a congenial exchange of observations that I could not refrain from remarking that nothing was missing but the coffee. My companion, the Right Reverend Monsignor Molz of Speyer, spoke of Barbara Pfister, the stigmatist, whose spiritual director he had been, but Therese, or Resl, as we now called her, in accordance with the custom, was not unduly impressed. She asked only whether Barbara Pfister, too, had been exposed to as many evil attacks as she was, and when assured that the number of them was probably even greater, she seemed wholly satisfied. If we speak of

Therese, she refers at once to "the dear Saviour," and what He wills she wills, and naught else. He knows how to manage all things; He is "so good" and "He can do all things." This is spoken so heartily, with such simplicity, without the least indication of pedantry, that soon it seemed to me, even, as something altogether natural and self-understood. Resl is exceptionally tactful. In order to give us opportunity for undisturbed conversation, she withdrew quietly to the kitchen for a while. She leaned on my arm, for the wounds of the feet compel her to hobble along on her heels. She has a word of hearty thanks for every little act of assistance.

When she had returned from the kitchen, Father Naber admitted a young newspaperman. We paid no attention to him, and so, with pencil poised, he questioned Therese. We noticed that his inquiries often missed their marks. Finally he summoned all his courage, and with the expectation of securing a private revelation at least for his paper, he asked her: "What would be your message to the world—expressed in three words—if you were to die at this moment?" The answer: "Nothing!" Bravo, Resl! said I to myself. You have just stood a severe test without knowing it. That was genuine humility and modesty. No, she does not consider herself called upon to leave a message to the world and to humanity.

We discuss newspaper articles concerning Resl. We mention those of Dr. Ewald of Erlangen, who testified to the truth after his personal experiences of many hours in Konnersreuth, only to reverse himself when he returned to the Erlangen atmosphere. Father Naber tells us that Therese had disclosed to him the spiritual condition of all those who have written against her, including Dr. Ewald, and that she had foretold what would come to pass.

Later Therese's parents came, and at once she arose

and took hold of her father's arm. There ensued a discussion between Father Naber and Herr Neumann as to whether Therese would return to her home for the night. It was understood that the fresh lime in the newly enlarged house would cause her great difficulty in breathing. Therese called attention to this, but without expressing her own will in the matter. The priest suggests that Therese remain at the rectory, but finally decides that she might make a test of her own home, and thereupon without any argument she followed her father, saying, "Whatever Father wishes." She drew her head-cloth closer about her face, because of the lurking photographers, and supported by her father, walked away gayly on her heels. (Arrived at home, she fell in a faint and Father Naber was called. Thereupon she was brought back to the rectory.)

Two hours had passed on swift wings, and then there was a hearty leave-taking. I would be lying if I were to say that Therese Neumann on this day made an especial, extraordinary impression upon me. There was no occasion for it. She moved in all things in a natural manner, her genuineness adapting itself to all circumstances. Of course, all of us were Catholics, and therefore as we sat about the table with Therese we were one heart and one soul; complete harmony of faith and spirit existed among us.

To these personal impressions of mine we shall add those of others, as contributions to an understanding of Therese's character and of the tests which the Church exacts in such cases as hers.

"I may have seen another person as far removed from any egotistical thoughts, but I have never seen one so remarkably free from all vanity," says Baron Aretin. "She has in nowise stepped beyond the natural boundaries of her being. In her own estimation she is still the servant-girl of 1918, and without the least desire to appear more than that. An old woman of the village lay dying, and without saying anything to anyone, but also without seeking to keep it a secret, Therese hobbled to the house of death so that she might, with tactful words, solace the last moments of the old woman."[68]

"The first impression was: This is beyond all doubt the most unassuming, the most upright and truthful child in the whole world.

"Time is precious, so I begin at once a considerate but searching inquiry. She is ready, for she understands that there are people who cannot comprehend her condition. But she does not understand that there are people who, despite their better convictions, do not wish to believe; people who would rather not know anything about God and religion; people who have an almost cultivated ill-will in advance against anything supernatural or extraordinary. Nor does she understand that there are people who dissemble, who do not hesitate to lie to one's face, and who cannot therefore give complete credence to an absolutely truthful being.

"Her answers are clear, ready, unaffected; all of her remarks sensible, in no manner contradictory. It is difficult to believe that she has had no further education than that of the primary school, through which she passed with only average grades; that she has scarcely read anything more than her daily devotions from the prayer book; that she has never been out in the world, and that her horizon has been bounded by the experiences of her home and family and her secluded native village."[69]

"Her father ... speaks now of buying a cow, and that is even more interesting to Therese. For she is a thorough, simple peasant maid, and to this day she delights in hearing talk of field and wood, cow and stable. She has read but little all her life, and of Anna Catherine

Emmerick—she did not so much as know the name."[70]

"It is, furthermore, a fact that Therese Neumann is not in the least high-strung, nervous, or neurotic; and that her piety is thoroughly wholesome. It may be of interest to know that she uses as a prayer book the Missal of Father Schott; and that she prays, in German, the prayers of the Mass which the priest recites rather loudly at the altar; that her first and last devotion, in addition to that of the Passion, is directed to the Blessed Trinity, and—this is remarkable in a simple peasant maid— particularly to the Holy Ghost."[71]

"I take my departure, but converse for a long time in the hall with the parish priest, who sees the emotional strain under which I am laboring. He tells me emphatically that Resl did not receive her stigmata as the result of being submerged in contemplation of a crucifix. I had intimated that this was possible. On the contrary, Resl no longer wished to look upon any pictures of the Saviour, because she found all of them defective and unreal. ... But all of this is nothing remarkable. The important, the most important thing is, the way Resl prays—how simply, how naturally, how heartily! As a child speaks to its father. She loves Our Lord's own prayer, the Our Father, best of all, and it moves one deeply to hear her pray it. There is in her praying more than can be told today. Something is in course of preparation, the culmination of which we cannot foresee."[72]

"She herself is convinced that what is happening to her is from above. But within her, strong and living, is the consciousness that this is not due to her own merits or powers, but only to the grace of God. Despite all the great things she has experienced, her humility cannot be disturbed in the least."[73]

"It weighs heavily in her favor that she is so childlike

in her obedience to her parish priest. I was favorably impressed, too, by a little incident at the beginning of our visit. Her mother had accompanied us up the stairs and was complaining because the physician had taken amiss the removal of a bandage. Therese said, 'Oh, Mother, please stop! I do not like to hear people talk about others.'"[74]

"To be a child in the sight of God and willingly and gladly conform to His will, that is the whole of her wisdom."[75]

"Be glad that you can be so close to the dear Saviour and serve His priests. Be sure to be very good, quiet, childlike, and modest, and remember always that the dear angels serve the Lord with you, and then He will be pleased with you."— Written by Therese Neumann in the prayer book of a Konnersreuth altar boy.[76]

"She never says a word about her participation in the sufferings of Christ. At the mention of suffering her attitude becomes one of pain and confusion. I asked her whether she had had a special devotion to the Passion, had meditated upon it.

Her friendly face became anxious, she looked at me with large, uncomprehending eyes, as though I spoke a strange language, and gazed questioningly and pleadingly at my companion. ... When I inquired whether she had read Anna Catherine Emmerick's works, she replied, 'No, I read very little.' In answer to a question as to how she spends the sleepless nights, she said, 'I pray.' And almost complainingly she added: 'But I cannot pray an entire rosary. I like best of all to pray the Our Father. And even at that I usually get stuck. When I say Father, I consider how God is our Father and all that He does, and I can't get ahead. God will have to consider the time and not how much I manage to pray!' I comforted her with the assurance that her way of praying was very good one."[77]

Baron Aretin says in regard to Therese in semiecstasy after the Friday suffering: "Her lips begin to speak, to express compassion with her Saviour, and her speech changes into a long and moving prayer, a peasant's presentation of all sorts of petitions for relatives and friends and persons who have asked her intercession for them. For herself she makes no request, save only that she be permitted to die. And all she says has this childlike refrain: 'But You are smarter than I am and You will know how to arrange everything for the best.' "[78]

"As though casually, I asked whether she desired to be freed from her suffering. 'O, no! In the beginning, yes; then it was hard for me to bear it, for it destroyed all my hopes. I wanted to become a Sister and go to the missions. But now I am glad to suffer. To suffer is now my vocation. We ought not to fear anything. Above all, do not fear! God has His plans for us when He allows us to suffer. It is true, what the Voice said to me, "More souls are saved through suffering than through the most brilliant sermons." For that reason we ought never to say we must suffer, but we are permitted to suffer.' "[79]

"At eight o'clock at night (on a Friday) Resl answered me when I called to her very loudly, but she did not know me, and finally said, 'Tomorrow, tomorrow.' The next morning, after she had received Holy Communion, I visited her again, for the parish priest had told her to tell me all concerning her interior life and all that I wished to know. We conversed for hours, and I observed her closely, as on Friday, and I could only verify the fact that she is the most childlike, the most simple soul I have ever encountered. She is in truth humble, obedient, lovable, and eager to meet the wishes of others. In short, she is like a child. ... For me the visit and the conversation with her constituted a rare treat. For ten years I have been laboring, through the magazine *Rosenhain,* to spread the spirit of childlikeness. The insight into this simple soul which it was given me to acquire has been a generous recompense for my labors, the more so because she grew up and became mature as a reader of *Rosenhain.*"[80]

IS THIS HUMILITY?

Are we justified in speaking, in the case of Therese Neumann, of the heights of mysticism? Were not all true stigmatists deeply, touchingly humble, and were they not eager to hide the signs of the crucified Saviour's wounds, so that in some instances their presence was not discovered until after the stigmatist's death? Can we imagine that Saint Francis of Assisi, if the thirteenth century had had the facilities of intercommunication which we possess, would have permitted himself to be a spectacle to thousands?

These questions have been raised. What is to be said in answer? Only this: "No and never!" as a reply to the question betrays a misconception of what humility means. Humility does not consist in hiding oneself in a dark corner, in shunning the daylight, for he who is highest in rank, who stands on the watchtower of the world, the Holy Father at Rome, can be as genuinely humble as the most obscure Carthusian monk. Humility is complete submission to the will of God. Was Saint Mary Frances of the Five Wounds the less humble because, at the command of her confessor, she displayed her stigmata publicly in a church in Naples? She obeyed and she humiliated herself utterly by permitting this spiritual ordeal to be exacted of

her. Had she refused, her humility would have changed
into self-will. Humility without obedience is not humility
but pride! And let us remember the words of Our Lord to
Sister Mary of Jesus Crucified: "The roses are for others,
but the thorns are for you!"

The important point to consider is this: Does Therese
Neumann, in permitting her stigmata and her Friday
ecstasies to be witnessed, consider her own desires? Does
she do this in order to acquire in men's sight the halo of
one especially favored by God; or does she act according to
the will of God as it is made known to her? The former
would not fit into the picture of her which we have drawn
as conscientiously as possible, and as other eyewitnesses
have seen and drawn it. The latter attitude is so correct
that only culpable ignorance could conceive of making it
a subject of reproach.

When Saint Margaret Mary Alacoque, encountering
opposition between a command received immediately from
Our Lord and one made by her confessor, asked the
Saviour what she was to do, the answer was, "Obey the
Church; that is, her representative!" We make this
reference particularly because Therese herself has said that
the Voice which spoke out of the Light on May 17, 1926,
the anniversary of the Little Flower's canonization, had
among other directions, told her how to conduct herself in
the matter of visits.[81] And Father Naber, in the first public
statement by him, declares: "We have no other object than
the honor of God and little Saint Thérèse, to whom the
invalid has for years been devoted, and the salvation of
souls. Finally, I should like to beg most earnestly that no
visits to the invalid, particularly lengthy ones, be made, the
more so ... because she prefers to be left alone."[82]

We have told how Therese in the beginning kept the
stigmata hidden and how the first ones and those which

came later were, against her wishes, brought to light and to the knowledge of her parents. The matter was spoken of in the village. Neighbors and acquaintances, whose request could not be refused, came and went, and so the tidings spread. Therese was concerned with one thing only: obedience to the priest who represents the Church! Therein lay, and still lies, the touchstone of her whole religious life.

The very first report by an outsider, and he not a Catholic, says plainly that Father Naber accompanied the visitor to Therese's room and that at the priest's request she showed him the marks of the Wounds.[83] Other witnesses corroborate the first report.

Johannes Mayrhofer declares that "Therese Neumann has a horror of everything extraordinary, of everything unusual. She would like best of all to be alone. She tried, though unsuccessfully, to hide the stigmata. ... But she would, best of all, like to be let alone. When a senseless person wrote that she ought to be put in jail or reformatory, she expressed her opinion with perfect complacency, 'There I could speak with God, too, and I would be free from visitors!' But in childlike obedience to the command from above and the advice of her spiritual director, she submits calmly and with friendliness to the many burdensome visits."[84]

Professor Naegle, of Prague, writes in July, 1926, two months later: "It is absolutely untrue that the nearest relatives of the girl or the parish priest or even the stigmatist herself have, as some newspapers have reported, desired to propagandize these extraordinary happenings. I myself saw how distasteful to her parents were the visits of so many curious people."[85]

"I wish to say emphatically that one of her most frequent gestures during the pauses in the ecstasies is to lock the door of the room and cause the people standing about to be dismissed. There can be no question of invitation or desire to attract attention," says Professor Wunderle in his report of August, 1926.[86]

"So far as I am concerned, they can put me in jail or hang me on the church steeple, if only God's holy will is done!" This is what Therese said, according to the statement of Father Wilhelm, S.J., in November, 1926. He continues: "When I took my departure, I advised her to have infinite patience, and to consider herself as an outdoor sign which must submit to wind and weather."[87]

After visiting Therese in November, 1926, Antonie von Taenzl wrote as follows: "Nothing is more painful for Resl than to have the attention of so many drawn to her. She has repeatedly told priests that she would gladly suffer all for God, if He would only take away the exceptional, that which attracts attention. She endures the 'sightseers' and the many visitors with patience and submission to God's will. She does not wish to cut herself off from the public, if the sight of her suffering leads some to God and to a better mode of life. The parish priest told me that since childhood Therese ... had always been demure, preferring to remain in the background."[88]

Cathedral Dean Kiefl's observation in December, 1926, was that the moral aspect of the stigmatist was as clear as crystal. The press, he says, has published many moving instances of this, including Therese's prayer, "Dear God, take all this away from me and let me be blind again!"[89] And Dr. Hollnsteiner says: "Her desire culminates in the prayer that the Saviour may permit her to suffer much, but such pain as others cannot see." (The prayer was uttered in the semiecstatic state.) "And on Thursday evening she said: 'If only the good God would arrange it so I could go about tomorrow, and all the people would wait in vain!'"[90]

Father Vogl of Altötting tells how, suddenly aware that contrary to her custom, her hands were not covered with linen bandages but that the wounds were exposed, she made a formal apology, saying that it was more comfortable this way. A critic—not an eyewitness—had written that she "wallows with delight in pain!" Father Vogl's testimony is of April, 1927. He says that Therese finds this necessity of permitting herself to be a spectacle, the most difficult of all her sufferings. With Father Naber's consent a place has been arranged for her back of the high altar of the village church. There, screened from the eyes of the curious, she receives Holy Communion. Her parents wish very much to obtain rest for their sorely afflicted daughter, but they always come to this conclusion: Father Naber must make the decision.[91]

Baron Aretin says Therese is "a peasant girl ... whom one can please best by totally ignoring what one knows of her experiences."[92]

R. Olden, writing in September, 1927, reports that the visits had become far too numerous, far too heavy a burden for Therese, and that she hoped the end of the vacation season would mean fewer visitors. But many are edified, Therese is told, and she retorts, not without sharpness, "Some ... some of them."[93]

Father Naber's own viewpoint is recorded by Karl Würzburger: "On the bridge between the thousands of visitors and the solitary girl stands the tireless parish priest, constantly wrestling with himself as to which is his higher duty, to lead the people across the bridge or to prevent them from crossing it. It is a perpetual contest in his conscience, and it has deep roots. He himself has told me of it, in substance as follows: 'It is true, we are offended by the curiosity of the people and we should like best of all not to admit anybody any more. But do we know what

God's intentions are in regard to Resl? It seems to me He wishes the people to learn something of the wonderful facts and events.' This attitude characterizes the whole situation in which Therese Neumann finds herself. In her true participation in the Passion she is shut off completely from the world, and if, on the edge of ecstasy, she becomes momentarily conscious of it, she seeks desperately to banish this disturbance of her sacred contemplation."[94]

The parish priest of Hasberg, Father Schilcher, writes as follows: "Father Naber, a quiet man, told me that at first he had persistently opposed the matter, but he realized now that God wished to accomplish something extraordinary. Smiling, I said to him, 'I would simply lock the door and send the people home.' But he answered with deep earnestness and with resignation: 'Resl has received a revelation that through her suffering many would be directed toward the other world, and so she must bear patiently what this brings with it. And neither do I wish to oppose it and offend against the will of God.' What more is there to be said?"[95]

Another eyewitness reports these significant words of Father Naber: "The girl lets the Lord do with her as He wills. We shall undertake nothing, neither shall we hinder anything. We wish to be the instruments of the Lord God, if He wishes to use us as such."[96]

Objections have been raised against Father Naber's standpoint in regard to making the charismata of Therese Neumann accessible to the public. A Professor Engert, of Regensburg, is of the opinion that this smacks too much of Port Royal. He depends upon a citation from the Scriptures to show that one ought to keep secret the mystical gifts of divine grace. But he proves too much, for the same citation might serve to prove that one ought to make God's works of wonder known and praise Him for them. *Sacramentum regis abscondere bonum est.* "For it is good to hide the secret of a king," said the Angel Raphael when he made himself known to Tobias. (Tobias 12:7.) And he added, "But honorable to reveal and confess the works of God," as if to furnish a reason why he thereupon disclosed the Almighty's designs and His merciful guidance. It is as though the angel wished to say that, while an earthly king's designs may be frustrated if they become prematurely known, this is not true of God's eternal and perfect plans. Indeed, it is "honorable to reveal and confess the works of God!"

One must not judge solely by appearances, even though one has seen and probed. An insight, a penetrating insight into the soul is essential. He is able to judge correctly and justly, before whom the soul lies like an open book; who has observed and shared; who knows how God has prepared the vessel of His election in the crucible of pain. Whosoever presumes to judge solely upon external evidence and then perhaps only to condemn, perhaps without having himself seen and tested the evidence, much less having even glimpsed the soul, is bidden to remember that there is a sin of false suspicion and of rash judgment. Even Therese Neumann is entitled to respect for her honor and her good name.[97]

We have endeavored, so far as possible, to direct the eyes of our readers to Therese's interior life; to help them know her as she is, as we found her to be. We have presented the testimony of many, truth-loving, competent persons who have seen and observed. We have done this so much that each reader might arrive at a preliminary, provisional judgment for himself. Let each one apply the tests from the viewpoint of the Church. Let him consider the presence of virtues and in what measure they abound: humility, obedience, prudence, faith, patience, love of neighbor, firmness, truthfulness, purity, and submission to the will of God. This is the manner in which the Church judges, and upon her findings she makes dependent the bestowal of the title of Blessed, which as generally understood implies the termination of the subject's earthly existence through death. The Church investigates with the purpose of ascertaining whether the Christian virtues have been practiced in an heroic degree. But this does not involve the practice of heroic virtue to a superhuman extent or by extraordinary means. Neither does it imply any special claim to or meriting of divine grace, since according to Catholic teaching, grace is not given because of human deserts but as an absolutely free gift of God. But perfection in the practice of virtue is attainable through "the ordinary, simple piety of a child," for precisely that constitutes the "little way of spiritual childhood" of little Saint Thérèse of the Infant Jesus, in imitation of whom Therese Neumann first entered upon the way and has steadfastly walked therein. The Voice always directed her along this path: "Obey your father confessor in blind obedience and trust him in all things. ... "You must die more and more to self! ..." "Remain childlike and simple!" "You need not fear, not even the interior suffering. It is only through suffering that you can cooperate in the saving of souls. Remain childlike in your simplicity. ..." "That you are so submissive pleases the Saviour!"

Pope Benedict XV, in his discourse of August 14, 1921, on the virtues of Sister Thérèse of the Infant Jesus, declared that in the little way of spiritual childhood lay "the secret of sanctity, not only for the French, but for all the Faithful scattered over the whole world. We have, therefore, every reason to hope that the example of the new French heroine will be the means of swelling the ranks of perfect Christians not only in her own country, but wherever the children of the Catholic Church are to be found."[98] And he reminds us of the words of Our Lord: "Amen, I say unto you, unless you be converted and become as little children you shall not enter into the kingdom of Heaven." (Matt. 18:3.)

Let us visualize Therese Neumann when, in the darkest moments of her painful hours, she was accorded the choice of restoration to health or the continuance of an invalidism of intense suffering, and spoke these words of strong faith: "Let it be done unto me according to the will of God! I am His handmaid and His child!"

Is such a prayer less than *heroic sanctity*? Is it not a proof of an heroic degree of virtue if one prays no more than this: "Father, if Thou wilt, remove this chalice from Me: but yet not My will, but Thine be done"? (Luke 22:42.)[99]

THE HIDDEN ASCENT

This chapter, so important as a contribution to the understanding of Therese Neumann, I owe to the pen of one peculiarly well equipped to write it by reason of his personal relationships and the receipt of confidential communications, oral and written.—*Author.*

I do not undertake to throw light upon the virtues of one still living, the stigmatized Therese Neumann, in order to present her as a saint, one whom we ought to or are permitted to venerate. I do so because she has been charged with fraud, and because it has been asserted that, instead of a wholesome interior life, she has during the seven years of her great suffering given herself to moody reflection, and that hallucinations have arisen. I consider myself in duty bound to comply with repeated requests that I set forth, so far as I am able, the truth about her life of virtue. I can present only the essentials. But I shall not depend upon what others have said or written, but upon what I myself have seen and heard during my several visits to Konnersreuth and conversations with Therese Neumann, and upon the many letters which she has sent me.

Even as a child, Therese was spiritually recollected and most of all determined to be very good and not to offend the dear Saviour. When she left her parents' house and entered the employ of a neighbor, her interior life developed rapidly, expressing itself especially in the simplicity of her conduct, in the modesty of her attire, abstinence from boisterous amusements, industry, and faithful discharge of all duties. She revealed an exceptional love of nature, delighting in birds and flowers. All of nature was the source of intense joy to her. All things reminded her of God the loving Father.

Therese harbored the earnest intention to enter a convent. She believed that God had called her to the religious life, and her father, who was called into army service in 1914, wrote to her again and again, that when the war was over she might enter the cloister, "if God wishes it." These words, "If God wishes it," draw themselves like a thread of gold through all of Therese's life. Early in life she had impressed upon her soul the desire to do God's will in all things. It surely was not easy for her to delay so long the fulfillment of her ardent desire for the religious life. But, as God wills. She could not leave her mother alone with all the younger brothers and sisters.

Since August, 1914, Therese Neumann had venerated Sister Thérèse of the Infant Jesus. A woman of his acquaintance gave Herr Neumann two small pictures of

Sister Thérèse of Lisieux when he was about to go off to war. As his eldest daughter was named Therese, he gave her the pictures, imagining that they were likenesses of her patron saint. But when Therese read the text on the reverse of the pictures, she found that this was another Thérèse. The friendly countenance of the Carmelite nun and the poetry on the reverse side of the card appealed so much to her that she went to Waldsassen, to ask the Franciscan hospital Sisters there (with whom she had for some time been in contact) to tell her more about Thérèse of the Infant Jesus. The Sisters gave her a copy of *The Story of a Soul*.[100] Henceforth Therese loved the little Thérèse very dearly and venerated her with fervor. With her small savings she purchased other literature concerning the Little Flower, and came to know "the little way," the way of spiritual childhood. She received a relic of Sister Thérèse, and this was for her an additional incentive to imitate the little Carmelite whose favor she was to experience repeatedly.

When I say that Therese Neumann venerated the Little Flower with fervor, I mean that she understood that veneration of her meant to imitate her. She hailed the appearance of a book, *The Secret of the King*, a practical introduction to the following of Sister Thérèse along the path of virtue; and despite her illness, Therese Neumann endeavored zealously to promote the distribution of this volume, so that many might come to know the little saint of Lisieux.

Blindness having come upon her, Therese Neumann's brothers and sisters read to her from *The Story of the Soul* and the other literature to which I have referred. Another book must be mentioned. Its title is *Up! Follow the Cross!*[101] Not a day passed but Therese meditated on a passage in this volume, which she wished might be placed in the hands of all who carry crosses, for none would complain of suffering if he read and considered what was written therein.

Even before her sickness, Therese led a genuinely interior life. Her letters prove this. The time has not yet come to divulge details. During her illness, her interior life developed constantly, becoming more and more perfect. Lying in her bed all day long, blind, unable to see and read, but undergoing extreme pain, she concerned herself, naturally, with the Divine Redeemer, in accordance with these books. She assured the Saviour, over and over, that she loved Him.

Father Naber, her confessor, had judged her interior life correctly and fostered her striving after perfection, prudently and effectively. He taught her to live always in the presence of God and recommended to her the frequent use of ejaculatory prayers. Her suffering prevented her from reciting longer prayers. Her favorite prayer, which she said with complete simplicity and interior fervor, was this: "My God and my All, what have I in Heaven, what do I love on earth excepting Thee, Thou GOD of my heart and my portion in eternity!" She often stressed the fact that this prayer, which she repeated many times during a day, contained all that she wished to say to the Divine Saviour.

At a parish mission in 1921, the missionary taught her this ejaculation: "Take me from myself and give me to Thyself!" These words taught her much, in particular that complete abandonment to the will of God which Thérèse of the Infant Jesus recommends, and the conquest of self. This ejaculation, Therese Neumann said, gives a sense of interior warmth. The magazine *Rosenhain* published an ascetical course which counseled its readers to adopt as an ejaculation a secret slogan which represents a summation of the individual's spiritual program. The short prayer was to be said often each day and become, so to speak, the breath of the soul. Therese pursued the ascetical course with intense interest and the closest attention. She writes explicitly that, with the approval of her confessor, she made the course in all earnestness. The confessor was of the opinion, however, that it afforded her nothing new. It is significant that Father Naber should have been of this opinion, for the course is a thorough one and grapples in no uncertain manner with the problems of the spiritual life. If it could not offer anything new to Therese, she must have traveled far along the path of perfection.

When still enjoying good health, Therese had used ejaculations as a sort of secret of her inner life. But she had not meditated so regularly on the secret and recited it often without reflecting seriously upon its content. The ascetical course led her to fix her attention upon the matter more fully, to use it, indeed, as the breath of the soul and thereby advance spiritually. She had chosen as her "secret" the phrase, "Everything to give joy to my dear Saviour!" As she believed she had a grave fault, this secret must now help her to combat it and wipe it out. She was inclined to become weary, discouraged; or, better said, out of patience, out of humor. There were things aplenty to tempt her in this direction. But now she would resist, asking herself whether it would give the Saviour joy if she were discouraged, impatient, and she answered the question for herself, and was quieted. She has throughout her life been intent upon pleasing her Redeemer. We know how even some of the greatest saints had to struggle with their temperaments, as for example, Saint Aloysius, Saint Ignatius of Loyola, and especially Saint Francis de Sales, whose outstanding virtue of meekness was achieved despite an exceptionally strong natural bent in the opposite direction.

In addition to ejaculation, Therese was devoted to novenas. She prayed much to Saint Thérèse of the Infant Jesus. But she never prayed for the restoration of her health. She always said: "I desire only what the dear Saviour wills. It is all the same to me, to be well or sick, to suffer or to be without pain. Not to cause pain to the Saviour, but to please Him, that is my desire." On the reverse of a picture which she gave to an acquaintance, she wrote this beautiful verse, indicative of her innermost conviction:

> I know that Thou my Father art,
> Within whose arms I'm sheltered well:
> I shall not ask how Thou dost lead
> But follow Thee with trusting heart.
> And if Thou gavest back to me
> My life, to use it as I would,
> I'd place it in Thy hands again,
> With childlike confidence in Thee.[102]

Surely, this reveals a high degree of heroism.

Therese Neumann endured her suffering, not only willingly, but joyfully. Her father confessor's counsel, the writings of the Little Flower, and especially *The Secret of the King,* led her to offer up her sufferings for the priests of the Church and the salvation of souls, in accordance with the statutes of the Theresian Children's Society, of which she was a member and promoter. She offered up her sufferings also to help others, who through their writings labored for the glory of God, the priesthood, and the conversion of sinners.[103]

Therese considers herself a bride of the crucified Christ. She considers her cross and pain the gifts of God to her. Whatever the Lord sends she gladly accepts. He is a loving Father and does all things for His children's welfare, even when He sends them suffering. ... Therefore, she wishes to be a bride of the Crucified. It helps her endure all that she must endure. Her vocation is to make sacrifices, to suffer, to renounce, to die to self. For this reason she has consecrated herself to the Sacred Heart as a sacrificial soul.

The apostolic element of an ardent zeal for souls is of necessity combined with the love of suffering and joy in suffering of this childlike, simple sacrificial soul. She expresses this in these words: "Oh, if only all people loved the Saviour! How wonderful that would be!" To a Catholic writer she said: "Be sure to write very much about the Saviour, about His sufferings, His love, and His mercy. ... We must lead all people to the Saviour, so that they may love Him! Oh, how that pleases Him!" She prays and sacrifices for priests, for good priests "who will please the Lord."

Atonement, too, has a place in her spiritual life, and in the spirit of Saint Paul. "I fill up ..." She says: "I add my sufferings to Thine, so that Thou mayest distribute them and all may come to love Thee." Her strength has been and still is the Most Blessed Sacrament, the nearness of which, at least occasionally, is felt by her. She has an ardent longing for the Holy Eucharist: "Daily I receive the Bread of the Strong, which I need so much.... For in addition to my sufferings, I have fierce spiritual battles to fight. ..." "Therefore also do not forget miserable me in your prayers. ..."

It hurt Therese when she discovered that young people behaved rudely, even sinfully, and in atonement she offered to the Heavenly Father the sufferings of Christ. She could not understand how people so often lack any appreciation of the good and the noble, how they can violate the holy peace of the night or even that of Sunday, by shouts and noise and unbecoming behavior.

Therese's love of nature manifested itself while she was blind and during her long illness. When her pain was not altogether too intense, she asked her brothers and sisters to arrange the flowers, of which she had quite a few, close to her. She herself, while blind, transplanted plants while in bed and more than once achieved a pretty mix-up. The song of her birds delighted her, and until she could no longer see, their bright feathers, too. How many half hours of meditation she owes to her flowers and birds! She saw in nature an image of the creative omnipotence of God, Who, like every artist, first conceives his work in his mind and then gives it concrete reality. In this she followed the great lover of nature and of God, Saint Francis of Assisi, who, in some of the most moving of all poems, greeted all creatures of God as his brothers and sisters, and glorified and adored the Creator by his love of His handiwork.

Ought not every pure soul be moved to think of the Creator, the generous and loving Father of Heaven and meditate on His attributes and thank Him with unselfish love, at the sight of nature's beauties, the flowers' glory of color and the marvelous clothing and melody of song birds? Keeping all this in mind, we must admit that Therese Neumann, a child of nature, an ardent lover of nature, did not indulge in phantastic daydreaming during her blindness and her invalidism. But remembering all the beauty she had seen in nature, she lived at all times in the most intimate union with the Bridegroom of her soul. It is He Who has given us all these things, and continues to give them, for our delight and edification.

This was the spirit in which Therese Neumann lived during her time of visitation. It is a monstrous error to believe that she felt unhappy. On the contrary, she declared some time ago that this was the happiest period of her life.

The chief characteristic of the interior life which Therese practiced during this hidden ascent of her soul, and which is reflected in her letters, is that simplicity which still animates her whole being and is undoubtedly the most amazing thing about her. The following words, which she wrote on a picture, throw a shining light on this quality of Therese:

"Make me simple, Saviour, simple as a child, so that in all things I may find naught but Thy love."[104]

As clear and as simple as this are her emotions and her expression of them, her thoughts, her meditations, her prayers. Hers is an artless and unspoiled naturalness, childlikeness, and this ought to give all of us the courage to attempt to imitate her, for all can see readily the possibility of imitation. She can in truth apply to herself the words of Holy Writ: "Which I have learned without guile, and communicate without envy, and her riches I hide not." (Wis. 7:13.)

And if we review her life today, considering all the extraordinary occurrences of the past two years, and her conscious action under grave responsibility in comparison with which the extraordinary things become of secondary importance, we come to the realization that it is a continuous commentary on the great commandment of Christ: "Thou shalt love the Lord thy God." In this commandment Therese combines asceticism and mysticism in beautiful harmony but wholly in the spirit of the admonition of Saint Francis de Sales: "Were we to become holy according to our own wills, we would probably never attain sanctity; we must become holy according to the will of God."

The majority of those who have thus far written about

Konnersreuth show no trace of an understanding of *this* Therese Neumann. Absorbed in their search among the basic stuffs of human life, they do not seem to see the rose which has sprung up and blossomed.

THERESE'S ECSTASIES OF THE PASSION

Konnersreuth, Friday, Aug. 26, 1927.

When we climbed the stairs in the Neumann cottage that morning, we heard that Therese was once more in an ecstasy of the Passion. It did not seem strange to me, but rather a thing to be expected. While we assisted at Holy Mass, with the consciousness of the nearness of God in an exceptional degree and with more than a usual experience of spiritual unity, Father Naber returned with the pyx, in which he had carried Holy Communion to Therese, and replaced it in the tabernacle. With the expectation that the day would make severe demands upon our nervous systems, we partook of a substantial breakfast, and then walked out to the village square. There was a long serpentine file of silent people waiting in the misty, cold morning air. They waited outside of the priest's residence, and each one's whole attention was directed to the room back of the two windows to the left of the door. After his Mass, which he had offered up for Therese, Monsignor Molz, our traveling companion, told us that he had been admitted at six o'clock and had witnessed the visions of the Scourging and the Crowning with Thorns.

At the moment in which we reached the steps leading to the rectory, Father Naber appeared, at first warding off the onrush, but at sight of us giving a gesture of friendly welcome. The door closes behind us and I am at the threshold of the room. Where the sofa stood yesterday, there now stands a bed, in which a woman is sitting upright. She is dressed in white, a blood-stained white headdress frames her face, and two broad streams of black, coagulated blood reach from her eyes, closed by the blood, down her cheeks and chin. Blood stains the white nightgown, particularly on the left side, under the heart, where a large, yellowish-red spot is seen. The hands, on which the stigmata stand out today in bold relief, are raised forward and upward, toward an object we cannot see. The countenance is as yellow as wax. The straining of the features, most of all the sharply contracted eyebrows, betrays a spiritual visioning and experiencing. I know it is Therese Neumann, but not because one would ever recognize in this almost ghostly being the young woman who had chatted with us so blithely the day before. The slight swaying of her upper body, her hands which are wrung in helpless pain, and then raise themselves again, in this direction and in that, as if wishing to take hold and help, all this is impressive and elevating in the highest degree. I allow the spectacle to work its way with me, and it leads me to the place where Therese now dwells, and to see what she sees, the Way of the Cross in Jerusalem. The picture which Therese presents is, for me at least, not overwhelming, though immeasurably impressive. What is overwhelming is her participation, for it is concentrated beyond her upon the object of her vision. I experience what Therese experiences: In this moment the Saviour is all, the surrounding background, even the people, including Therese, are unimportant accompaniments, trivial matters, as Therese herself says when, during the pauses between ecstasies, one questions her. Time disappears. All is in the present tense and the year 33 A.D.

is the apex between past and future.

The ecstasy is a complete one, a wholly, exclusively supernatural seeing. Therese is withdrawn from the entire created universe, and so our entrance does not disturb her in the least. Chairs are brought and from our position near the door, unobserved by those outdoors, we can see Therese at close range. The room is heated, the stove glows, and Frau Neumann comes and goes about the bed of her Resl.

Now the ecstatic sinks back into her pillows. Her hands lie upon the featherbed that is spread over her. She struggles for breath, moans faintly. If her mother or Father Naber asks whether the pain is intense, the answer invariably has reference to Our Lord, to the suffering Redeemer. For Him are her touching, childlike whispers of compassion, never for herself.

Suddenly there appears before the eyes of her soul one of the nearly sixty visions, each of which comes to her not as a dead picture, but as a living reality in which she has part. Her upper body rises from the bed, her hands resume their raised posture. She is enrapt.

Towards eleven o'clock in the forenoon Therese complains that it is frightfully hot, as the procession of the cross-bearing Saviour, in which she follows Him, has now passed from the shade of the houses of Jerusalem. Again and again her hands clutch at the marks of the crown of thorns, as though she would pull out thorns which have penetrated deeper and caused more pain than the others.

As noon approaches, Frau Neumann sprinkles water on the floor to cool the air. During one of the pauses, when we went into the next room or from there into the kitchen, I saw the visitors departing through the garden. They had been permitted to look at Therese for a few seconds through the open door. Deep earnestness is upon the faces of most of them. Women weep, some of them cannot understand the matter. Their countenances betray their consternation. I did not see a single one who was entirely indifferent, unaffected. Father Naber spends the entire morning at the door, regulating the human stream so that each individual may catch a glimpse of the stigmatist. He does this work with infinite patience. At a quarter to twelve, with the cry, "The Crucifixion begins," he dismisses the spectators and closes the rectory door. Only the priests, of whom many have remained for this specific purpose, are allowed to stand in the door, each one for five minutes.

The Crucifixion of Our Lord does in truth begin. We see it in the mirror of Therese's ecstatic vision. Her slender hands, yellow as wax, are raised up, and the stigmata on the palms lie as if in deep furrows. Under the agony of the nailing the hands twitch continuously and her thin fingers contract. Her tongue seeks in vain for moisture on her lips; her head falls forward and her mouth licks the sponge raised to it, but turns aside with a gesture of experienced bitterness. Now Therese's head is raised up in a listening attitude, to the left; that is, to the right side of the Saviour and to the thief crucified there. Her pain fades for a moment, for she hears, with visible joy, the words of the penitent: "Lord, remember me when Thou shalt come into Thy kingdom!" Then she hearkens towards the Saviour, to catch His reply, but turns suddenly with an angry look away from the curses of the impenitent thief, the "bad man," as she calls him when asked about him. It is now about twelve-thirty o'clock. I draw the attention of Monsignor Molz to my left, to the change in Therese's countenance. Only pain had been mirrored there, but now it turns ashen-gray, almost gray-blue, her cheeks have become cavernous, her face is drawn lengthwise, her mouth becomes smaller. Involuntarily my lips form the words: "My Lord and my

God, up there on the Cross, forgive me, too, for Thou didst die for me and my transgressions!" That was truly an act of perfect contrition, and this alone would have been ample recompense for the inconveniences of the visit to Konnersreuth. Now, with a jerk, a last terrible spasm passes over Therese's body, from her feet upwards. There is a final summoning of the last remnants of strength—and in the same instant, so quickly that one could not notice details, Therese falls back upon her bed, heavily as a stone, and her hands drop to the coverlet. It is consummated!

With an emotion of relief because Therese has survived her bitter agony, and with heartfelt thanks to Father Naber, we leave the house and return to the year 1927 out in the world. It is five minutes to one o'clock.

❦❦❦

Have I exaggerated, have I allowed myself to be carried away by my feelings? Two citations, of which non-Catholics are the authors, are submitted for comparison. They may serve to amplify my account.

Dr. Reismann says: "When I see her again the next morning she is a picture which no one who has seen it will ever forget. A girl's form is raised from the bed, the upper body rigidly erect, the arms outstretched imploringly. The wounds of her hands glow. Her face is distorted by immeasurable pain. She wrings her pale little hands as though her heart were breaking. And her heart does break; long since the blood from it has stained all the coverings.

"This girl weeps blood! From the painfully closed eyes there issues blood, a few drops only at first, but finally there are two wide streams that flow the full width of the cheeks. A thousand impressions are mirrored in the distorted features. Terrible happenings are grooved in this strained, listening face. Her body jerks, shudders, for she experiences the scourging of Our Lord, and suddenly, when the jailors press the crown of thorns down upon the head of Christ—the wounds of her head are opened and color the headcloth blood-red! Tortured, she clutches at her head, to pull out the thorns, again and again."[105]

Dr. W. von Weisl, who is not a Christian, makes this report:

"I gaze and gaze. In front of me, upright in the bed, is a picture of woe. An aged face stares enraptured into vacancy, paying no attention to us standing about. The mouth half opened, the hands stretched helplessly forward wish to grasp something. They clutch but encounter space, and withdraw draw themselves with a gesture of despair and are crossed over the breast. And the eyes—never before had I seen such eyes! No hysteric, no insane person, has such eyes: agonized, horrified, her swollen, blood-incrusted lids are turned to her visions, which only these closed eyes behold! These eyes see more than our open eyes. And red, red, red drops of tears are on her cheeks. There were six or seven long stripes of blood on the left cheek towards ten o'clock; on the other cheek the number was much less. But in the afternoon both eyes are submerged in the same blood; blood streams are coagulated on cheeks and chin and jaws, down to the neck. Bloody tears color even the chemise.

"The ecstatic weeps blood. And on her outstretched hands, which are colorless as faded ivory, gleam two red marks in high relief: the nail-wounds of the Saviour! ..."[106]

The Catholic's innate consciousness of Friday as the day on which Christ was crucified and died, does not cause the organic flow which, it has been asserted, plays a part in the phenomenon described. This is shown by the manner in which the ecstasies begin. They come upon Therese unawares. She is, so to speak, ambushed, surprised by them. On the Friday within the Octave of the Assumption she expected them so confidently that she invited the Reverend Dr. Stegmann of Heilbronn, who had inquired about them, to extend his visit until then. But there was no ecstasy of the Passion. They have, in the cases of other stigmatists, failed to come during this week of joy in Heaven.

A respected non-Catholic tells how he sat, with Father Naber, at Therese's bedside, beginning at 9:30 at night, to make his observations. They talked of indifferent matters and she herself chatted gayly and with animation about the ravens of the cathedral at Bamberg. "Suddenly, in the middle of a sentence, Therese ceases to talk. She raises herself up in her bed, her eyes gaze out into space. All the outward signs of an ecstasy appeared. Astounded, I looked at my own watch. It was three minutes before twelve o'clock, midnight."[107]

Once more we ask: Are these visions of the Passion a product of the imagination? If they were, after two years, after week upon week, their effects could not possibly be what they are. The imaginative faculty would have been exhausted long before this, so that it would no longer be able to receive any impression at all. For it must not be forgotten that each Friday, as her descriptions show, Therese sees exactly the same thing, even down to minute details. Even the most terrible spectacle, seen again and again, week after week, through two years, will lose its potency, will fail to elicit reaction, cannot possibly continue to move the beholder to bloody tears. But the impression upon Therese and her capacity to be impressed continues to be as great, as intense as they were on the first day, without the least diminution or weakening, without becoming matter-of-course, but with the same effect. Does this lie beyond the border line between the natural and the preternatural? Only the body of Therese Neumann is utterly exhausted, to the point of collapse. It is a spectacle of indescribable pain.

A problem worthy of investigation is this: Does Therese in her Friday ecstasies suffer actual physical pain? All indications of it are present. It is sufficient to see her when she witnesses the scourging, the crowning with thorns, or the crucifixion. One cannot but conclude that all the indications point to this as a fact. Yet, one can press Therese's hand with the stigma and there will not be the least reaction, the least sign of pain, whereas in her normal condition the wounds are very sensitive. I saw how, during one of the ecstasies, her left arm fell swiftly and struck the edge of the bed, whereupon an expression of severe pain was immediately reflected in her face. I incline to the opinion that the sufferings of her ecstasies are agonies of the soul with echoes in the physical frame. As a matter of fact, the phenomena which cause the suffering do not originate in the natural sphere of the physical and material; no earthly being is at hand to press the crown of thorns upon this brow, and yet, when the soul sees the crowning, its natural result is manifested on her head. One may say, therefore, that during the ecstasies the body is not responsive to sensations derived from the natural order. Experience shows that, at times, the body is not subject to natural laws and fails to react to natural stimuli. Bernadette Soubirous, the Maid of Lourdes, inadvertently held her hands for several minutes in a candle flame without being harmed at all. No longer in ecstasy, she cried out in pain when the flame was brought too near her hand.

After her ecstasy vision of the scourging, Gemma

Galgani bore the marks of bloody stripes visibly on her body. On the second Friday of March the flesh was slashed, on the third Friday to such an extent that one could almost see the bones, and on the fourth Friday there were wounds on her whole body. They were about one centimeter deep. After two or three days they disappeared.

One would expect that, in the circumstances, Therese would live in constant fear and dread of what the ecstasies inevitably bring upon her. Dr. Reismann saw her again on that Thursday evening, when after their conversation she walked "with us from the rectory to the home of her parents. She appeared as calm as ever," he writes, "though every fiber in her must have been anticipating what was to come in a few hours."[108] The Reverend Dr. Stegmann asked her whether she feared or desired the Friday Passion ecstasies. She said "she really did not know what to say in answer to that question." He repeated the question, asking her whether she was filled with dread as Friday approached. Her answer was, "Not that." He wished, then, to know whether she awaited Friday with joyous anticipation. "No, that neither." It was, she declared, a matter of indifference to her, if only God's will be done. Such a complete surrender to the Divine Will is, of course, beyond the comprehension of a worldling. It is that "perfect rest in the heart of the Source of all being, with which," as the convert Monsignor Robert Hugh Benson writes, "God will one day reward His children throughout eternity."

What was it Therese said to Otto Timmerman? "Suffering is now my vocation. We ought not to fear anything. Above all, fear nothing!" And to us she said, "I do not fear God, I love Him!" She told Baron Aretin that the years of her blindness had been the happiest of her life. "I was a witness, on this and on other days, of her atoning endurance of pain and of her absolute devotion to Christ and her willingness to suffer according to His will."[109] Dr. von Weisl marvels at her "patience in suffering, which is at once so great a grace of God and so heavy a cross." She nods energetically: "Yes, it is a heavy cross and a great grace!" Therese possesses a desire to suffer. Colossal foolishness, sheer insanity, is the verdict of the world which flees from pain. And some Catholics share this opinion. There was once a great saint, John of the Cross, whom Pope Pius XI recently proclaimed a Doctor of the Church. He was one of the most important Catholic mystics. Once, as he lay praying before a crucifix, he heard a voice saying: "John, what wilt thou have of Me for the service thou hast done Me?" Unhesitatingly, he answered, "Lord, naught but suffering and to be despised for Thy sake."

Do men gather figs from thistles? May we judge a tree by its fruits? Go to the Saviour—that is the burden of all of Therese Neumann's statements. But what do some people expect of her? One, writing in a Berlin newspaper, is amazed because the ecstasies are not contagious; because no ecstatic symptoms have appeared among those who have gazed upon her. No one weeps, cries out, sinks upon his knees on these Fridays! Ought we to look for such effects?

"To bring about miraculous cures is the last thing that would occur to her, and anyone who seeks such things in Konnersreuth is sure to be completely disappointed. But a conversation with the girl of Konnersreuth, who has been tested in the crucible of pain and is willing to suffer, a conversation with her on the nature and value of suffering, is one of the supreme experiences of life," says Otto Timmerman, who has visited her several times.[110] "Among the thousands who came to Konnersreuth after Easter,

some returned home thinking seriously of what they had
seen. They may have arrived in the village with a skeptical
smile, and carried with them up the narrow stairs to the
girl's room, all the armor of modern 'enlightenment.' But
after standing in the circle of spectators around Therese's
bed, they were strangely uncomfortable, and they gave
themselves to earnest thinking as they left the little house
and they walked silently back to the place whence they
had come."[111] "It was the most impressive, the most deeply
moving experience of my life."[112]

A Jesuit says that Therese recounted with intense joy
that she had managed to accomplish some good. "More
than one who had for a long time absented himself from
the Sacraments had been converted. I heard of a man who
had not been to confession for ten years, but who, on the
first morning after his visit to Konnersreuth, visited the
tribunal of penance."[113] "To very many the phenomena of
Therese Neumann have been the impulse toward opening
their hearts to the grace of belief."[114] "The case of Therese
Neumann indicates, at all events, a religious impulse of
unexpected power."[115]

Such testimony as this explains the frothing anger and
the ravings of the Communists, which are heard from as
far away as Russia.[116] Hell is in an uproar. "A few weeks
ago a stranger asked permission to visit Resl in the
afternoon. To the parish priest's amazement, Therese said,
'Let him come! I have something to say to him.' And when
the stranger stood beside her bed, Resl said to him, without
opening her eyes: 'Here is one who does not love the dear
Saviour; but neither does our Saviour love him!' And then
she told him of certain grave offenses he had committed
and declared that he came from Russia. One of those
present recognized him by what she had said and testified
to the accuracy of her statements. It is not difficult to

imagine how chagrined the man (who had changed his station in life) went away."[117]

Another reports that while he stood amid the waiting throng and listened to the pilgrims' conversation, there was some excitement in the crowd. Something had happened! A man had come from Therese's room. She had said to him, "You are an unbeliever, go away!" And he left at once, climbed into his automobile and drove off.[118] (According to a Vienna report of non-Catholic origin, the man in this case was the most notorious Hamburg atheist, Drews.)

Faithful to our intention not to render a decision of our own, we close this brief chapter with the words of the well-known free-thinker of Jena, the publisher Diedrich: "At last a breach by the supernatural through the walls of our materialistic world!"[119]

THE STATE OF EXALTED REST

Konnersreuth, August 26, 1927.
(Friday evening)

At half-past six o'clock we returned, at the invitation of Father Naber, to his home, at the door of which some twenty persons waited. We were admitted at once. Therese lay as when we last saw her at one o'clock, blood-drenched, sunk deep into her pillows, pale as a corpse. Her condition is the same as during the intervals between the morning's ecstasies. She reacts to the questioning of the priest, but her intellectual response is that of a little child. Her face is turned somewhat toward the wall, her eyes are still closed by the thick, black incrusted blood, and the wound marks of her slender, colorless hands are uncovered. Father Naber turns on an exceptionally strong light, so that we may see well. He takes his place beside the bed and we sit close by.

"Resl, do you know me? I am *der Herr Pfarrer* (the pastor). Resl, child of the Saviour, have you suffered much?"

She answers in brief phrases, with pauses between them, as a child does, and her voice is very low, but readily heard, particularly by me, as I have been familiar with her dialect since my youth. Her thoughts are still centered on what she had seen during the forenoon. "—dead, dead, I felt so sorry for Him. He could scarcely get up again when He fell." The dialogue turns to the reasons for Christ's Passion. Therese, too, is one of the sinners for whom He suffered, is the burden of her words now. "The Saviour helped me again. ... I caused Him sorrow ... took it all away again." She tells that she offered up this day's pain for Father Naber, in appreciation of the hospitality he had given her.

We speak of the Cross. She has declared genuine two particles of the Cross in Father Naber's possession, and indicated the portions of the sacred wood from which they came. One splinter, she said, was from the spot where the Redeemer's right forearm touched the Cross. Monsignor Molz draws forth a little cross wrapped in paper. It contains two particles which had been carried by Barbara Pfister, the stigmatist, until her death. Therese does not see what is taking place. But when the parish priest holds the little cross close to her lips, they frame themselves instantly to kiss it; her fingers grasp for it and play with it caressingly. "Oh, this is something good! This is from the wood on which the Saviour hung, where His back touched it!" She indicated that Monsignor Molz owned the cross and declared that it had been in the possession of the "maid" (Barbara Pfister), who has been with Our Lord for a long time, who was permitted to suffer very much, "just like me. The people were not good then as they are now." She is now with Jesus, and she needed only to "pass through" Purgatory. With her is another "maid," who was also permitted to suffer very much, and who went "directly to Heaven." We knew that she meant Anna Catherine Emmerick, and Dr. Mut questions Therese concerning the beatification of this stigmatist. But it requires considerable maneuvering to make this matter comprehensible to Therese. The concept of Pope is unknown to her while she is in this state. Therefore Father Naber says to her, "Resl, you know who I am. I am your pastor." "Yes." "Above me is another, higher pastor, the bishop." "Yes." "And above him is still another, the highest, the great pastor, the Pope." "Yes." "And what do you think, Resl, will this highest, greatest pastor soon say something concerning this 'maid'?" Her answer is: "He will say something, but not much. The next one will say nothing. But the next one, he will say a lot! Do you know, there was one who wrote down what the 'maid' said, but he wrote some of his own matter into it, too, and now they do not know what is what."

Let it be said in explanation that Barbara Pfister in her childhood visions often saw Anna Catherine Emmerick. Later in her life, Anna Catherine visited her and consoled and counseled her when an exceptionally severe suffering came. And as is well known, the Sacred Congregation of Rites of the Roman curia decided in May, 1927, that the visions of Anna Catherine Emmerick can bear no weight in the process of her beatification, because it is now impossible to determine what part of the records are original and what parts are the additions of Clemens Brentano, the German Romantic.

In regard to another particle of the True Cross, Therese

declared that it had been taken from the Cross during the reign of Pius X. Of course, she does not mention this Pope by his name, but designates him as the "highest pastor who was before the one who was the last to die." She said of Pius X that he "is already in Heaven. The Saviour loved him very much, because he labored so hard that Our Lord might come to so many. He went straight into Heaven." She verified our belief that she meant the decree of Pius X fostering frequent Holy Communion, and that this Pontiff would be declared blessed. The Pope as head of the Church, as Vicar of Christ, the concept of him as Pope, she expresses by calling him the successor of "the one who cut off Malchus' ear," and "who was there when the cock crew so loudly," two scenes in which Saint Peter played the chief roles and which make a strong impression upon her during the Passion ecstasies.

In regard to one whom we shall not name, Therese said, if my memory serves me correctly, that she has been in Purgatory for twenty years. At this Father Naber said, "What, such a long time?" Whereupon Therese said to him, "You talk almost stupidly today. 'A long time!'—there is no such thing in eternity!" And as there is no concept of time in eternity, her answer was theologically correct.

Now Dr. Mut puts in her hand a relic of Contardo Ferrini, who was a friend of Pope Pius XI. "This is of a man who loved Our Lord very much. He is already in Heaven with the dear Saviour. He knew the highest pastor very well; he wrote a lot which Our Lord told him to write." Asked as to the possible early beatification of Ferrini, she gave the answer which she frequently gives, "The Saviour did not tell me that." This was her reply, too, when asked whether Our Lord would soon call two persons specified by the inquirer.

A third relic is offered to her. It is of the Little Flower

of Jesus. She greets it as she would a beloved friend. "O, I know her well! This 'maid' has come to me, often." She tells how she was cured of her blindness and how the injured vertebrae were healed. "But she has scolded me, too! Of course, she may do that. And you, too, Father (Naber). She tells me what to do so that it will please Our Lord." In reply to the question, "Have you ever displeased Our Lord?" she confessed that she had, but added that He had "taken it all away again." *Tollit peccata mundi!* She tells how Saint Thérèse of the Infant Jesus had healed the open bedsores, instantly, by "pulling the skin together again." Father Naber inquired, as if amazed: "But Resl, can she do so much?" Promptly came the answer: "She? Why, she can do nothing! She goes to the Saviour, tells Him, and then does what He tells her to do!" Unconventional, but theologically unobjectionable! For such is the doctrine of the Church concerning the intercession of the saints.

Concerning her vision of the discovery of the True Cross, Therese told us that the Jews had taken down the crosses soon after the Crucifixion and cut all of the longer beams into two pieces, so that the crosses of the two thieves (in T-form) were now in three sections, while that of the Redeemer (in the form of the Greek Ψ or Y, with an elongated upper beam) was now in four sections. The concepts of the numbers three and four were foreign to her, and she spoke of "one piece, and one, and one, and one." "That is, four?" she was asked. "I do not know. One and one and one and one!" The timbers, Therese related, were buried in a deep trench and then a house was built above the whole, but of that she did not dare to think. (It was a temple of Venus, and Therese's face expressed extreme disgust and annoyance.) Later the house fell into ruins, and the whole was a mass of debris until a "high lady" came with many men and women who dug into the trench and found the crosses. That of the impenitent thief had rotted away, could not be found. The other two were well preserved. How did one recognize them? Reluctantly Therese answered that the sections still fitted together and the Cross of the Saviour had been of a different, harder wood. Three sick persons were brought forward, two women and a man. One of the three was blind. As soon as they touched the Cross of Christ they were healed.

There are still, Therese declares, three large pieces of the True Cross in existence: one is where the "highest pastor" is. (She evidently means the large portion of Santa Croce in Gerusalemme in Rome.) Another section the "high lady" took with her and it still exists, but one does not know where. The whereabouts of this section and of the third part "the Saviour has not told me." At the Last Judgment, she continued, all the particles of the Cross will be reassembled, for "the Lord can do all things." It will appear high in the heavens, shining brightly, especially at the places of the nails. Under the Cross the Saviour will appear, surrounded by many "bright, shining men" (angels), and then will come the separation of the good and the bad. There is "lots of room" in Heaven, says Therese, and it is beautiful there, because the Saviour is there. She is of the opinion that she would not care to go to Heaven if He were not there, and at this declaration her mouth makes a grimace of contempt. She wishes to go only where Our Lord is. At the Last Judgment people will be "whole," that is, consist of body and soul. She anticipates it with joy. "Many things will happen then!" And she herself? The Saviour will come and take her, but not "all"—something will remain there (she points with a hand toward the graveyard). As to whether the "something" will remain there, "The Lord did not tell me ... but when He takes me I will come for you, too, soon, very soon!"

Meanwhile Therese's mother had entered the room and after removing the blood-drenched headcloth, she began to talk with her daughter. Therese tells how the Saviour had to suffer and the mother listens the while she washes the incrusted blood from Therese's face, and consoles the girl as only a mother can console her child.

It is nearly 9:30 at night when we leave the rectory, deeply impressed by what we have seen and experienced. A few words more concerning this ecstatic condition, which some call the intermediate state, because while it lasts the physical senses are awake and open to impressions. Accept the state of rapture as the border line, across which the body united with the soul in rapture seems to be drawn, now to a lesser, now to a greater extent. One might also compare a person in ecstasy with a room which has two windows, in opposite walls. Now one window is opened or closed, now the other. These are, however, mere aids toward understanding the condition of the ecstatic. A truer analogy is this: The ecstatic is drawn, to a greater or lesser degree, into the supernatural world, and since God's will is the only law in that domain, this can take place only if He wills it. It is a matter, therefore, of man being seized by the Kingdom of God: Thy Kingdom come! But we must not imagine the supernatural world as something whose distance from us can be measured in kilometers. No, the Kingdom of God is about us, it permeates our whole world, as though the latter were not concrete, actual. For this reason, no man can penetrate the supernatural realm so far as his body is concerned unless he is physically withdrawn from this world or from the place in which he is. No rules can be applied to this matter, as to the extent to which an ecstatic in varying circumstances may be caught up and rapt in soul, for no rules can bind the will of God, which operates herein as it wishes.

DEPARTURE FROM KONNERSREUTH

August 27, 1927 (Saturday)

Konnersreuth extends hearty hospitality to the thousands who, drawn by Therese Neumann, come to the village. Many of the visitors remain a number of days. Not only do the people accept no remuneration beyond their actual expenses, but they often accommodate people, particularly priests, without accepting anything at all. Father Naber especially gives, without any recompense whatever, his time and his great patience; more than one of those whose words have been written down in this book was his guest for days, and never was there the least indication of a desire for gain. (It is a characteristically Communistic-Socialistic slander to say that "the priests heap up money" at Konnersreuth.) And Therese's parents, too, refuse absolutely to accept any donations. I was glad that at least the picture which I brought along and which was my wife's handiwork, was accepted.

We were eating breakfast in our quarters, after Holy Mass, when the door opened and my good friend, Otto Timmerman, entered. Returning from Geneva, he had made the detour to see Therese and us. With him, we went to the rectory to say good-by. In the course of an exchange of views with Father Naber, the idea of writing this book was born. Then we went into the room in which Therese has been lying since yesterday. I am the first one to enter. From the white pillow she smiles at me. Her face is still pale, but it is once more the countenance I knew before the

Friday ordeal. Her childlike guileless eyes laugh merrily, and she puts forth her slender hands on which the stigmata are darkly red. "I thank you very much for the beautiful picture. Father Naber showed it to me early this morning. Do you know, it is a true likeness of the dear Saviour? That is exactly the way He looks, especially the forehead and the eyes, exactly as His are. Only the beard is somewhat different, it has two peaks. And with a man that makes a difference, but in all other respects ..." She sends heartfelt greetings to my wife and my two children, and a promise of her prayers is her farewell to me.

"Onkel" Mut's departure is brief and hearty. Characteristic of him were the last words of our venerable prelate: "Resl, pay heed to what I tell you, the hardest is still to come! It will come soon, very soon, for you have already gone far. It is the night of the soul, the abandonment by God. You shall call upon Him and He will not answer." And she tells him: "Yes, it has already begun, but it does not last long." To which he adds: "Barbara Pfister endured it for eleven years! But you need not be fearful. Just obey Father Naber, and now, good-by, God have you in His keeping!" And Therese says: "As God wills. It is all the same to me!" She waves her hand in farewell. We leave Konnersreuth.

Everyone who has seen Therese early on a Friday afternoon, shortly after the mystical death; who has seen that wan, agonized countenance, as pale as a corpse, and that bloody body, will tell himself that, normally and according to nature, her recovery must be a matter of weeks, nay, of months. And any man who has experienced one such crisis will consider it amply sufficient for his whole life. That he could undergo a second one, after only a few days' interval, is highly improbable. But on this Saturday Therese's face was once more filled out, although still pale. In the afternoon she was able, as usual, to arise and by evening she was, as I was informed, restored to the degree of health in which we had seen her the preceding Thursday evening. And this despite the fact that she has for several years eaten nothing at all, nor taken even a drop of fluid. And for two years there has taken place regularly the change whereby her weight decreases on Friday but on Saturday is increased by the amount that was lost. In the natural order of things, she must long since have been reduced to a skeleton, if she managed to live at all. Whence this strength? Whence the recovery in the short space of one day? And how is it that the terrible experience leaves no trace upon her spirit, so that Therese is on Saturday her natural self again, merry as a child, calm, patient, and free from any of the consequences which one might expect, most of all in the nerves. Thus far I have encountered no attempt to explain this riddle of nature. The facts exist. They are incontrovertible. They have been verified by thousands.

THE ECCLESIASTICAL AUTHORITIES AND KONNERSREUTH

From the time he made his earliest reports to them, the ecclesiastical authorities of the Diocese of Regensburg counseled Father Naber to exercise the utmost care and circumspection in Therese Neumann's case. They did not wish to hinder either earnest investigation nor the visits of individuals, and they have placed the greatest reserve upon themselves.

Of the German bishops, the Right Reverend Dr. Schreiber of Meissen convinced himself by becoming an eyewitness. In September, 1927, the bishops of Bavaria, at their annual conference at Freising, issued a most earnest admonition "not to render a final verdict in the Konnersreuth case until there has been a decision by the authorities of the Church. Therefore all visits ought to be omitted." This "earnest admonition" was followed on October 4, 1927, by the following declaration of the Regensburg ordinariate:

The Episcopal Ordinariate of Regensburg makes known in the official publication of the Diocese of Regensburg:

This year's conference of the Bishops of Bavaria has adopted the following resolution:

The Bishops of Bavaria in Conference at Freising herewith issue a most earnest admonition not to render a final verdict in the Konnersreuth case until there has been a decision by the authorities of the Church. Therefore all visits ought to be omitted, as the Bishop of Regensburg has from the first requested. The press is requested to reprint this announcement.

This resolution takes no stand on the occurrences at Konnersreuth. It was necessary to prevent the establishment of a sort of pilgrimage place, before the matter received ecclesiastical authorization; and it was even more necessary in order to forestall those of ill will who would, basing their declarations on the fact that they had visited Konnersreuth, issue false reports, write with unauthorized pens about things which they do not understand in the least, spread errors and blaspheme all that is supernatural and sacred. Nor was it impossible that the hostile agitation aroused by the strange happenings would in time lead to dreadful consequences, to deeds of violence even, in Konnersreuth. All this is forestalled by the resolution, and if many earnest, well-meaning Christians must make renunciations, their sacrifices are not futile.

Meanwhile the ecclesiastical investigation proceeds, quietly and with certainty. Four Mallersdorfer Franciscan Sisters especially qualified for the purpose, were selected to test the total abstinence from food, liquid as well as solid, on the part of Therese Neumann. The Sisters kept a continuous, uninterrupted vigil of fifteen days, day and night, after having taken oath before an episcopal commission that they would perform their task with the utmost conscientiousness and entirely according to the directions of the physician in charge, Sanitätsrat Dr. Seidl of Waldsassen, Then they spent two days at Waldsassen, to receive special instructions from Dr. Seidl. They began their work at Konnersreuth by making a thorough search of Therese's room. The eyes of two Sisters were at all times upon the stigmatist; she was weighed regularly; the water used to cleanse the mouth was measured before and after its use. Blood from the flowing wounds and also from an incision in the earlap was sent to laboratories for testing, to ascertain whether it was hunger blood. Other chemical investigations were made, too. Tests were made along a number of lines. All of them yielded the same result. It was proved that Therese did not partake of the least bit of food of any kind.

During this vigil Therese, by no means exceptionally thin, was not always confined to her bed, but arose, remained in her room, went to the village church or to the next house. Amazing was the further fact that, despite the complete abstinence, in two instances considerable loss in weight was followed by a subsequent increase of about the same amount.

Dr. Seidl made nine visits during the fifteen days' test. Twice he arrived in Konnersreuth at night, unannounced. Occasionally he brought with him Dr. Ewald, professor at the University of Erlangen. When the four Sisters had completed their task, for the conscientious performance of which they received the highest medical praise, they again took oaths before the episcopal commission. The comprehensive report by Dr. Seidl, with a supplementary report by Dr. Ewald, and the diaries of the four Sisters, compel the admission that the test could not have been more rigorous, more scientific, and could not have yielded any other result, if it had been conducted in a hospital or in a clinic. The latter was desired but could not be carried out.

The basis furnished by natural science as a result of this investigation, is no more than a foundation on which to conduct a philosophico-theological inquiry.

The reverend clergy, which may make what use it desires of the foregoing, will exert its influence to prevent further visits to Konnersreuth. An earnest admonition by the episcopacy will be accepted by Catholics as binding in conscience.

Regensburg, Oct. 4, 1927.

Dr. Scheglmann, Vicar General.

Wuehrl, Secretary.

Professor Ewald, of Erlangen, saw fit, again in this case, to change his position afterwards.

Archbishop Dr. Hauck (who is not the Ordinary of Regensburg) at a Catholic meeting in Nuremberg called, in a measure, upon Therese's parents to meet the request of ecclesiastical authorities that their daughter be placed in a clinic for observation. He went even further than to suggest this. According to the regulations established by Pope Benedict XIV, this cannot be demanded of Therese nor of her parents; and as to the abstinence from food, her oath would satisfy the Church completely. Therese's father

is keenly conscious of his responsibility toward his child
and refuses to surrender her into strangers' hands and
have her withdrawn from his protection. In his sermon
entitled "Seven Principles Concerning Konnersreuth,"
Cardinal von Faulhaber reports that when she was advised
that she was of legal age and no longer subject to the will
of her parents, Therese replied: "The dear Saviour was
subject to His parents until His thirtieth year."

On October 29, the capitular vicar of the Diocese of
Regensburg expressed "the earnest and urgent wish that,
in consideration of the general interests of the Church and
of Therese's health, all visiting cease."

As this "earnest and urgent wish" was that of the
temporary administrator of the diocese during the vacancy
of the See, and therefore not a decree with the character of
a local ecclesiastical ordinance, there existed no sort of
obligation to abstain from visits to Konnersreuth; and, in
fact, they have taken place daily, in uninterrupted
sequence, and the visitors are always admitted if they
produce a written permit issued by the Regensburg
chancery.

In September, 1928, the conference of the Bavarian
bishops issued a proclamation sanctioning this procedure
and permitting it to be continued. The proclamation says:

"A year ago, visits to Therese Neumann in
Konnersreuth were made contingent upon special
permission of the episcopal ordinariate of Regensburg,
because of the throngs which gathered there and also
because of abuses. The parish of Konnersreuth and the
Neumann family have accepted this regulation in pious
obedience to the Church, and have, so far as they were
able, observed it. The visits of large numbers of people to
Konnersreuth are to be avoided, as heretofore, because
sensationalism and curiosity have no place there. The

clergy will in particular observe this regulation. Only when special and sufficient reasons exist that justify an individual visit, can the required permission be sought from the ordinariate. Applications must be accompanied by the recommendation of the applicant's parish priest."

Chapter VI
CONCLUSION

W E approach the end of our task. There remains only to consider the significance of the facts which we have set forth.

Their chief significance is, of course, for Therese Neumann herself. That all the aspirations of her soul are directed solely toward God seems to us an incontestable fact. An exact investigation would be possible, however, only to her father confessor. All others can do no more than make conjectures. But we should like to indicate, briefly, the bases of such spiritual progress as Therese Neumann has made. For the reason given, we dare not presume to undertake an application of the principles. We shall depend upon a thoroughly reliable guide, a Saint and Doctor of the Church, John of the Cross, and his work, *The Dark Night of the Soul.*

When the soul begins to ascend the heights of mysticism, there is at first a twofold process, the Godward yearning of the soul and the attraction of the soul to Himself on the part of God. The process varies in details, according to the peculiar endowments of each soul and according to the specific purposes which God has in drawing the soul to Him.

There is essential and inescapable in this process a purgation through suffering, as a means of atonement and of fashioning the soul so that it may enjoy union with the infinite majesty of God. While the soul which has been separated from the body needs but a cleansing of the spirit in Purgatory, the mystical ascent demands a purgation of the senses also. Most of all, there must be a purification of desires, an uprooting of all taste for earthly things, whereby these lose their power of attraction. This is necessary because, so long as an inclination to earthly things remains through the senses, the soul by virtue of the perfect union of body and soul necessarily shares in that inclination. The soul must be purged of all attraction for things of the senses in order to be able to enjoy perfect union with God.

This liberation of the spirit requires violence. It is painful. For God cuts away what is bad, removes all that hinders the ascent, while the soul on its part, by exercising its power of will, casts off the incrustations of earth and abstains from anything that might hinder the union.

The nature of the soul makes it imperative that God mold it to His purpose, and its weakness makes possible only a slow and gradual healing and sanctification, which consists of both a spiritual deepening and strengthening. The liberation is achieved slowly, as a child achieves adult stature slowly. With it come changes in perceptions, judgments, and love, and the painful process is correctly termed an "upheaval of the cosmic order" by Dr. von Weisl. The perspective of Konnersreuth enabled him to understand its necessity.

To the cleansing of the senses there must be added the cleansing of the spirit through its liberation from natural tendencies, so that its taste for higher values may be unhampered and the soul made free to consort with the Divine Wisdom. This purgation is accomplished by the filling of the soul with divine light.

In his renowned vision of Domenico Savio, Blessed Don Bosco asked him: "Is this light supernatural? Is it light from paradise?" He was told that it was a purely natural light, but revivified by the omnipotence of God. When Don

Bosco asked whether one might catch a gleam of supernatural light, he was told that no mortal could see this light until he comes to the vision of God, for even the faintest ray of that light would cause a human being, an earthly creature, to die instantly. Then Don Bosco asked whether there were a light even more beautiful than that which illumined the vision, and Domenico Savio said to him: "Certainly there is. ... Look!" Don Bosco tells how he lifted up his eyes then and recognized a beam of infinite smallness at a great distance, but it was so dazzling that he closed his eyes and cried out. His cry awakened Don Lemoyne, who was asleep in the next room. That tiny, distant ray was more than one hundred thousand times brighter than the light of the sun and had sufficed to light up the whole created universe. When he opened his eyes again after some minutes, he asked Savio what it had been—a glimmer, perhaps, of the eternal light? "No, even that is not the supernatural light, although in comparison with natural light, it excels the other in brightness. If an infinite ocean of the light, of which you saw a single tiny beam from afar, filled the universe, you would still have no conception of the glory and beauty of the light of paradise."

The purgation of the spirit by the divine light is exceedingly painful. The naturally weak soul is unable to grasp it and bear it. It is dazed, blinded, and believes therefore, at first, that it is submerged in darkness and night. This blinding of the eyes of the spirit is the "night of the soul." It is felt as a frightful pressure, an inconceivably heavy weight. To this is added the state which makes any support by the senses impossible, and in which the being is plunged into an absolute vacuum; and the effect is such a realization of the soul's own nothingness that there ensue discouragement and despair bordering on the unendurable. The condition which the divine light brings about is therefore correctly considered as a parallel to the process of disintegration of a dead body. The spiritual blindness brings in its train a feeling of terror at the immeasurable distance from God, a sense of being rejected, of spiritual death; but at the same time, because God has laid His hand upon the soul, it experiences confidence in His mercy, love, and justice. More and more the soul becomes aware of the purgation's progress. Its eyes that had been blinded open gradually, accommodate themselves by degrees to the divine light; its love increases, and it is now capable of realizing the greatness of God in all His attributes. Not until this has been accomplished can it achieve, in the full mystical sense, a complete fulfillment of the Great Commandment to love God with the whole heart, the whole soul and all strength. Nothing hinders love, now, and the soul is in a certain measure dehumanized and made divine. The "veils have fallen" and the soul can be united with God, if He so wills. It is in a state pleasing to God, and as it is still united to the body and is still a creature of this world, and therefore able to act and earn merit, God employs it for specific purposes, most of all in the interest of the Church.

We know that Therese Neumann, following friendly counsel, long since began to offer her sufferings for the priests of the Church, thereby supplying what they are lacking in grace and which prevents their efforts from achieving complete success. Doubtless, Therese's ascent was made easier for her because she had begun so early to walk in the way of spiritual childhood, in imitation of the Little Flower. This had preserved her to a very great extent from the worldliness to which others often succumb before they begin the ascent later in life. And the secluded village of Konnersreuth fostered the required predisposition. The "world" does not lure in that little hamlet. The most beautiful things there are the village church and God's nature. But despite this we must not take it for granted that her way to God has thus far been an easy one to tread.

Another significance of the Konnersreuth case is the one it has for us, chiefly because of the example which Therese Neumann gives us. She seeks first the Kingdom of God. If we do that, too, all else will be added unto us. Therese teaches us to have absolute confidence in God, and therefore, a pure faith in Him; and a spiritual renewal in prayer. Therese shows us by her example what we ought to be and what we ought not to be, according to the desire and will of the Church, in order to be perfect Catholics. In this regard, the year and a half during which Therese was visited by tens of thousands, have already brought many blessings and have exceeded the best parish mission in the depth and extent of their effects. Many pastors have told us that this is true and I myself am conscious that I owe much, very much, to Therese Neumann.

This leads us to a consideration of the third significance, that for the world at large, which in these days to a great extent no longer believes in God, is steeped in unbelief and therefore in sin, or wanders in error. Konnersreuth has been fruitful in many circles, has fructified the seeds of faith in many souls, faith in the personal, living God of love and justice, and as a consequence, of punishment. It has, as Cardinal von Faulhaber declared in his sermon on Konnersreuth, again confirmed belief in the immortality of the soul. It has restored a meaning to suffering, demonstrating that it is a blessing and not a curse. Konnersreuth has advanced the cause of idealism immeasurably and has struck telling blows at materialism. It has affected our praying, hitherto so exterior and superficial, and has deepened it, revivified it, and placed the Saviour once more in the center of our spiritual lives.

And from afar all may today see that this is true: Therese Neumann is the product of an exclusively Catholic soil. To imitate her is to walk a path which leads inevitably to the Catholic Church. Of course, we shall scarcely manage to achieve the stigmata, though the gate to them is open. But another stigma awaits each of us on the Day of Judgment, the vision of which Therese Neumann has told us of in semiecstatic state: the stigma of the Lamb with which the angel of God will mark the elect, or the sign of the Beast. But from the latter may God deliver us!

APPENDIX

Feast of Our Lady of Lourdes, 1928

OUR months have passed, since I wrote the foregoing chapter and with it completed this book; four months which will be, in the history of the future, a scarcely perceptible space of time. But they have been eventful in the life of Therese Neumann. They have been significant, most of all because of the desperate attempts to silence the voice of conscience which Konnersreuth awakens in so many. This voice must be silenced at all costs, and the means adopted has been to act as though the case were ended, and as though the curtain of history had been lowered once for all and the drama of Konnersreuth were a thing of the past. Konnersreuth, it is asserted, has nothing more to say to the people of today, who have been so uncomfortably stirred up by it. And what it has said, one was confident, would be smothered beneath the avalanche of daily papers pouring by the millions from rotary presses.

Employing evidence which does no honor to him as a man of science, and which warrants the suspicion of other motives than pure love of truth, Privy Counselor Ewald has once more defended his thesis of hysteria. However, to make his theory applicable to Therese Neumann, he was first compelled to place the whole of humanity, with the exception naturally of the psychiatrists, in the category of hysterics. Father Geiger, rector of the cathedral of Bamberg, has brought Dr. Ewald to judgment in his rejoinder to the Erlangen professor.[120]

A Dr. Koerner, writing in a weekly medical-scientific review, allowed Therese Neumann's organism to become a sort of living nitrogen plant by means of which she draws nourishment in atoms out of the ether. And thus is her "apparent" abstinence from food explained! This is the capitulation at once of science, common sense, and sincerity.

The more vulgar implements of falsehood and slander are used by the Socialistic and Communistic press in its personal attacks upon the stigmatist, but in the courts it met defeat upon defeat, and with them sentences of fine and imprisonment.[121] The arbitrary and transitory production of a few bloody spots through intentional disturbance of the circulation of the blood, and this done for an admission price, has been set forth as "a solution of the riddle of Konnersreuth." He who offers this solution admits, honestly, that it has nothing to do with the Neumann case.[122]

In short, all possible means are resorted to, in an effort to discredit the phenomena of Konnersreuth, to silence the voices which speak of a Divine Hand at work there. Despite all this, the phenomena continue to take place as hitherto, and we have no occasion to change even a line of our book as this new edition appears; much less to retract anything we have said. At most, we might accuse ourselves of an excess of caution, of reserve, here and there. Daily it becomes plainer that at last, in circles which kept aloof in doubt, a change is taking place, a turning in the direction in which we felt it our duty to lead the way.

As was to be expected, the episcopal regulation which, for the time being, allows only such visitors as obtain special permits from the Regensburg diocesan authorities, has been religiously obeyed at Konnersreuth; and reliable information concerning events since then is limited chiefly to a small group of persons. There has never been a complete ban on visits to Konnersreuth, and one hears of eminent personages of our own and of foreign lands, among them the Right Reverend Joseph Schrembs, Bishop of Cleveland, Ohio, and the Norwegian Protestant theologian, Dr. Kristian Schjeldrup, being admitted to the Neumann cottage. Not a single trustworthy report of anything that Therese has said offers us the least warrant for retractions; all of them confirm our standpoint. And so we shall submit reliable accounts of what has since then happened to her and in connection with her case.

The marks of the Wounds remain unchanged. Their disappearance would not, however, be a proof that they had not been genuine, for they have been bestowed upon some stigmatists for a limited time only. It is probable that we would find, if it were possible to make the necessary investigation, that all stigmatists implored Our Lord to take away the outward signs and increase the hidden pain, so that they would not appear as privileged beings in the eyes of the world. Sister Columba Schonath, O. Pr., when she made this petition, was answered thus by the Saviour: "Art thou ashamed to bear My marks? Not for thy sake, but for the sake of the world shall they be made manifest. …"

As in previous years, so also in this year, 1928, the Friday Passion ecstasies did not take place during the Church's season of joy, from Christmas until Septuagesima Sunday. But with the beginning of the ecclesiastical pre-Lent, that is, as early as Friday, February 3, and Friday, February 10, Therese once more witnessed the Redeemer's agony in the garden and His capture there, and her heart and eyes bled again. On the Friday after Ash Wednesday she began once more to see the entire Passion, culminating in the Crucifixion; and on the Sacred Heart Friday of

March, the second day of the month, as always on this privileged day, her vision's content was the piercing of the Heart of Christ. On March 9, while in ecstasy, she declared that the chair reserved for her use back of the altar of the village church, might be removed, as she would be unable to go to church until Easter. The total abstinence from either solid or liquid food continues. Since September, 1927, she no longer swallows even the few drops of water which it was necessary for her to take to consume the particle of the Sacred Species. Now she is able to receive an entire Host, which, placed upon her tongue, disappears instantly, though neither her mouth nor the throat muscles move in the least.[123]

When she receives Holy Communion she sees Our Lord Himself, and His sacramental presence remains with her until a short time before the next Communion. Since Christmas, 1927, she has seen Our Lord in the form of the glorified Christ-Child during Mass, from the moment of Consecration, when His real presence begins, until the Communion, as also when she receives the Body of her Redeemer and when Benediction of the Most Blessed Sacrament is given.

What has been the physical condition of Therese Neumann during these four months? She is not actually sick, but she suffers intensely, especially for others. She suffered most of all during the recent carnival season preceding Lent. During the night between the Saturday and Sunday before Ash Wednesday, when the world was giving itself to abandoned pleasure and heaped sin upon sin, she experienced a terrible ordeal. She was at this time a guest at the rectory. At the parish Mass on February 19, Father Naber gave his people a detailed account of the agonies endured by her at this time. She lay in the room in which we saw her on August 27, 1927, during her Passion-ecstasy. Above her bed hung a large carved crucifix, which Father Naber had purchased before his priestly ordination, intending it for his own home when he should become a parish priest. While Therese lay in an ecstasy, the Christ freed His right arm from the Cross, stretched it over her, and looked at her with such compassion and wistfulness that she began to weep bitterly. Father Naber, at the sight of her, was moved to tears, too. Again she offered herself as a sacrifice of atonement for mankind. And on the same morning, at the reception of Holy Communion, she saw Our Lord sweat blood in the Garden of Gethsemane, and in a supplementary picture she saw the dancing and jubilant world, women in shameless attire, indifferent to the Saviour and His Cross. Therese suffered beyond description for the sins of that night. She suffers also constantly for individuals, for the poor souls, and of late for a certain public sinner who is near to death.

But the period was rich, too, in consoling visions. A priest who was privileged to look deep into the soul of Therese enables us to report further concerning her vision on August 10 of the martyrdom of Saint Lawrence. She described it to him in a most detailed manner, and what astonished him most of all was this: that she who had never learned any ancient or modern foreign tongue, reproduced exactly, in Latin, the words of Saint Lawrence to his judge, as they are set forth in the Roman Breviary.[124]

On September 17, 1927, on which the Church commemorated the stigmatization of Saint Francis of Assisi, Therese beheld the entire process of this miracle of divine love. On the anniversary of the death of the Little Flower, which fell on a Friday, it was expected that Therese's heavenly helper and friend would manifest herself. And so she did. When at night the first picture of the Passion presented itself, the familiar Light appeared

and the Voice spoke, but in addition to this she saw the
Saint for the first time, saw her as she appeared on earth.
The Little Flower announced to her that she need not
suffer any more that day, but ought not to receive any
visitors until noon.

The Feast of All Saints, November 1, brought Therese
a vision of heaven with Christ and His angels and saints.
The next day, the Feast of All Souls, her vision was of
purgatory; and on December 8, of the Immaculate
Conception. On Christmas Eve she saw the preparations
which were made for the birth of Christ. She saw Mary
and Joseph seek in vain for a room at the inn and turn
finally to the stable. Towards midnight she saw the Saviour
as a child in the manger. On December 26, she was present,
in vision, at the trial of Saint Stephen the Proto-Martyr,
before the high council, and at his stoning. On December
27, the Feast of Saint John the Beloved Disciple, she saw
him at the Last Supper and at his death. On the Feast of the
Holy Innocents she had visions of Herod's decree that the
children be murdered and of the actual slaughter of the
innocents. She declared that fifty-five children of
Bethlehem and nineteen of the immediate vicinity had
been killed. At eight o'clock that night she witnessed the
death of Saint Francis de Sales, who died on that day in the
year 1622 at Lyons. On January 1 the subject of her vision
was the Circumcision of Our Lord, and on the
corresponding subsequent days the finding of the Boy
Jesus in the temple and the wedding feast at Cana. On
January 20 she saw the martyrdom of Saint Agnes; and
that of Saint Sebastian in all its details. She saw Saint
Sebastian pierced by arrows, and restored, confront the
Roman emperor. On January 26, in harmony with the
Gospel of the Sunday, she saw the temptation of Christ.

Despite her manifold sufferings, Therese is

astonishingly fresh and cheerful. When her strength seems about to fail, when her condition seems desperate, the nearness of the Saviour is made manifest to her and she enters into the state of "exalted rest," as she herself called it while in ecstasy, and from this she emerges with strength renewed. While she is in this state, the veils of the past, of the present, and of the future seem to be drawn aside for her. The Saviour permits her to know things that are secret, and experience has taught us that we may rely upon the fulfillment of all that she foretells while in this condition.

Ever since it became widely known that Therese possesses the faculty of discerning relics (hierognosis), she has been bothered by the receipt of an immense number of them, submitted to her for tests of their genuineness. This ought not to continue.

An occurrence which can now be made public, because one of the chief participants has himself told of it, is the visit to Konnersreuth of the Right Reverend Bishop Schrembs of Cleveland. On his *ad limina* visit to Rome in 1927, he came to Bavaria, his native land, in December of that year, and reports as follows concerning his conversation with Therese Neumann:

"During this time very few persons were in the room because no person now is allowed to see her without permission of the Bishop of Ratisbon. There used to be thousands who passed her bed during the hours of her torment, but the Diocesan authorities put an end to this. So when we were there, with the exception of Father McFadden and myself, there was nobody present but the pastor, a soldier at the door, and the father of the girl. The mother would come in and go out. You couldn't tell when she came in unless she happened to stand in front of you, she was so silent. When the girl was having an ecstatic vision the mother might go and stand beside her daughter's bed and smooth out the pillow so when the girl sank back exhausted she would have at least a little more comfort.

"At this particular time, eleven o'clock, the mother happened to be standing near me. Now, the girl hadn't known the mother was there. I hadn't known it, but the girl, coming back from her vision, suddenly spoke to her mother.

" 'Mother, dear, you know that man who is sitting next to you (that was myself), he comes from this country. He used to live round about here, but now he lives in the far distant land across the big water, and oh,' she said, 'oh, he works so hard, he spends himself without thought or care to his health. He works so much for Our Lord,' (and for my consolation she added), 'and Our Lord loves him very much. And you know, Mother, I have something to say to him, but I can only say it to him all alone. You must all leave the room.'

"So everybody started to leave the room. Father McFadden was sitting near. Of course, he has the disadvantage of not understanding what was going on, except when I would interpret it. He rose and turned to go toward the door, when the girl spoke to me and said, 'Oh, no. That other man that is sitting next to you, he can stay. It won't matter. He won't understand anything anyhow.'

"So Father McFadden came back and he became the only witness to that strange conversation that took place between that girl and myself. For three-quarters of an hour that girl reached into the innermost depths of my soul. She told me things that remained locked in my breast, but that I cannot forget to my dying day. She spoke even of conditions of my Diocese. She delineated certain things to me concerning the persons with whom I daily work. She described some persons so minutely that I could place my fingers on them and know exactly whom she was talking about. Father McFadden was the only witness to it. He saw the effect it had on me, as I knelt more than once in tears.

"And then suddenly she started back and the visions came to her again."[125]

The extraordinary abundance of incidents during the last six months compels us to forego the recording of any further ones, and to deal with them in a subsequent volume, which will carry forward the story of Konnersreuth.

After the Friday ecstasies and the suffering which they entail had once more reached their climax during the Holy Week of 1928 they ceased for an interval, until the Feast of the Sacred Heart, June 15. Therese had been told that the ecstasies and the pain would be resumed on that day. Thereafter there were only such interruptions as coincided with the Church's liturgy, as on the Feasts of the Assumption, of St. Lawrence, patron of the Konnersreuth church, and the nativity of the Blessed Virgin.

From July 19 to 21, with the same companions as in 1927, we visited Konnersreuth once more. We were able to see Therese and converse with her for hours. The impression upon us was the same as that made upon us the previous year. Outwardly, she has grown somewhat older, so that she appears to be what she is, thirty years of age. The Right Reverend Bishop Dr. Waitz of Feldkirch, in whose company we were, has written extensively concerning this matter, in his book, *The Message of Konnersreuth.*[126]

The number of visitors on Fridays continued to range from 100 to 150 people, among whom priests predominated. On March 23 and again toward the end of April, there came to Konnersreuth, at the direction of His

Holiness the Pope, the Franciscan Father Gemelli, rector of the Catholic University of Milan, a specialist in the field of medicine and psychiatry, and one who had once fought in the ranks of Socialism. "He conducted his investigation with the utmost care," writes Bishop Waitz, "and has declared most emphatically that there is not the least trace of hysteria on the part of Therese and that there is no merely natural explanation of her spiritual state. He, who has investigated dozens of strange cases and has uncovered more than one fraud, spoke with the utmost appreciation of Konnersreuth."[127]

Following Father Gemelli's personal report to the Holy Father concerning Konnersreuth, His Holiness, under date of May 3, sent his blessing to Therese Neumann and Father Naber.

A man of science who enjoys a wide and solid reputation because of his scientific attainments and his critical ability, Father Alois Mager, O.S.B., of Beuron, professor at the University of Salzburg, has written extensively, too, of his visit to Konnersreuth and has not withheld the expression of his convictions. Concerning the stigma, which he examined, he says that "anyone who studies it must admit that it does not look like a natural wound. It is neither a wound in the process of being naturally healed, nor a wound in the making. No inflammation of any kind, no reddish coloring is visible on the flesh immediately about the wound. ... Therese Neumann's whole behavior, her actions and her speech, gave me the firm conviction that she is a personality which is not deceived and still less deceives others. She is an honest and noble, deeply pious and childlike being. This impression will never be effaced from my mind."[128]

Concerning the Friday ecstasy Father Alois says, in the same report: "The spectacle has nothing repulsive, nothing violent, or awkward. I saw the Passion Play at Oberammergau. It was gripping, and tears ran from the eyes of thousands. But what was that play in comparison with what I saw at Konnersreuth? ... It happened that I was present when she told a Franciscan priest, who was a missionary in Brazil for many years, but had now been in Europe for some time, that he would return to Brazil and have much to suffer there. Unforgettable for me is the Sixth Station, at which Veronica wipes the face of Jesus. An indescribable glow of joy floods Therese's face, because she finds at last a compassionate soul which does a service of love for the Redeemer."

Later Father Alois visited Therese while she was in "the state of exalted rest." He found her changed in the most amazing manner. She lay there with a face that was transfigured, with a soft glow of health, peacefully and with closed eyes. "It seemed as though she had not undergone the terrible ordeal of which we had been witnesses throughout the long morning. ... As she continued to lie there with closed eyes, I believed it necessary to tell her who I was. But when I told her I was one of the Fathers from Salzburg, she said, 'I knew you were.' Then she unfolded with baffling accuracy a rather detailed picture of my work as a religious, priest and teacher. I was astonished at the minute knowledge which she displayed. Again and again she emphasized the fact that not she but the Saviour was saying these things, and that later she would be unable to recall what she now told me. My astonishment increased when she gave an exact analysis of the state of my health and declared that the physician in Munich, by whom I had been examined during the Christmas holidays, had not correctly understood my condition. She spoke in a similarly accurate manner of my intimately personal affairs."

This Benedictine of Beuron sums up his verdict as follows: "If I consider the occurrences at Konnersreuth as a whole, as a phenomenon consisting of many separate factors, I cannot escape the personal conviction that these are happenings which cannot be explained, at any rate exclusively so, by any natural means. There is at work here a preternatural, or rather a supernatural power. ... That the natural faculties of the soul have any part in the phenomena is out of the question, so far as I am concerned, because they alone never suffice to produce stigmata in this sense. The chief factor must be a supernatural energy. ... My personal conviction is that the process is miraculous. A divine work beyond the ordinary channels of grace is operative in this soul. ... It is my honest conviction that supernatural and miraculously divine forces are the causes of the Konnersreuth happenings." Finally, Father Alois speaks in opposition to further scientific investigation in a clinic and sets forth his reasons for taking this position.

Meanwhile, an increasing number of bishops have visited Konnersreuth. His Eminence Cardinal von Faulhaber appeared on the eve of the Bavarian episcopate's conference at Freising. He did not only remain at the bedside of the stigmatist from Thursday night until Friday afternoon, but on the following morning he offered up the Holy Sacrifice of the Mass in her room and gave her Holy Communion.

On his way back from the conference, Bishop Sebastian of Speyer came to Konnersreuth. The new Bishop of Regensburg, a few days after taking possession of his See, visited Therese Neumann.

Other members of the episcopate who visited the little village of the stigmatist were Archbishop Count Zichy of Kalocza, the Right Reverends Dr. Schreiber of Meisen, Kilian of Limburg, O'Rourke of Danzig, Waitz of Feldkirch,

Gross of Leitmeritz (repeatedly), and Malan of Petrolina, Brazil. Almost all of them very kindly gave us reports of their impressions, and their conclusions are unanimously favorable. Indeed, they are far more than that.

The summer before, Therese Neumann had told her spiritual director that all which had happened until then was but a preparation for what was to come, what God had decreed. What are His designs? We are unable to make even a conjecture. But Dr. Hynek, of Prague, is in a position to report that one who was incurably sick, and who had been recommended to Therese's intercession, was suddenly cured in a wonderful manner.[129] Already one non-Christian has, at Therese's bedside, found the true faith and received Baptism in the village church. She has seen souls which have been released from purgatory through her vicarious suffering; and from several sources there have come to us reports of extraordinary graces received by those who had begged Therese to intercede for them.

However, if Therese's mission were already realized, her task finished, the blessings which it has brought upon the earth would be so manifold that we should not be able to express our thanks for them. But the *caeterum censeo,* the admonition which we borrow from Therese and desire to sound forth in this book, is this: May all men finally believe again in the Divine Saviour's love and mercy, and turn to Him with confidence, for, as the stigmatist of Konnersreuth tells us, "He is *so* good!"

EPILOGUE

The author's account ends with the state of Therese Neumann's condition in 1936. She would eventually die of cardiac arrest on 18 September, 1962.

Apart from the mystical accounts that the author has defended in these pages, the servant of God also caused conversions, particularly of one agnostic former protestant, the journalist Fritz Gerlich. Gerlich visited Konnersreuth with a mind to expose her as a fraud. Instead, he was deeply moved, and returned frequently to speak with her, and transcribed several of her visions, eventually writing a 2 volume work; on 29 September 1931, he entered the Catholic Church, taking the name of Michael. Gerlich was a writer for the *Munich Post* (*Münchener Neueste Nachrichten*), and was among the earliest voices against Hitler's rise. His written work against the Nazis was not merely a fruit of his own foresight, but was inspired directly by his visits to the stigmatist of Konnersreuth.

The witness of Fritz Gerlich has confounded his secular biographer, Ron Rosenbaum (*Explaining Hitler*), who tries to explain it away, assuring his readers that Therese Neumann was indeed a fraud, and Gerlich must have had something wrong with him—never mind that he continued to write excellent articles, and was one of the very bravest of the early anti-Hitler circle. It was his newfound Catholic faith and encouragement from Therese Neumann that gave him the strength to attempt to found a new publication against the nascent Third Reich, which led to his arrest and martyrdom at Dachau on 30 June, 1934—the Night of the Long Knives.

The subtitle of this book is *A Stigmatist of Our Day*, and that is as true for us in the 21st century as it was in the

1930s. If one looks at articles on the internet, or the Wikipedia page, skeptics, even the ones addressed by von Lama in this work, are prominently displayed giving us the impression that "science" has concluded that she was a fraud, as if defenses such as von Lama's and others had not been written. Yet "science" has today devolved to the point where it doesn't seem to know what a man or a woman is!

In an age of hyper-rational post-modernism, where so much has changed in both Church and state, it is important to remember that the miraculous still takes place, and also amidst great suffering.

To modern people, the sight of a suffering woman provokes the thought, why would God allow such pain to be inflicted on a young woman? The saints, especially St. Thérèse of Lisieux, to whom our stigmatist was so devoted, embraced the redemptive power of suffering. An agnostic like Fritz Gerlich saw this suffering, and did what his rationalist colleagues found unthinkable.

Modern people, however, shrink from suffering any loss of their appetites, even many Catholics. These things are old fashioned, we suppose, or they're for other people. While certainly the extraordinary quality of the sufferings of a Thérèse of Lisieux, or a Therese Neumann are not what God has destined for each of us, just the same, inflamed by that same spirit, we can pull just a little of that redemptive suffering into our own lives, whether we are dying of a painful illness, or suffering a headache, uniting ourselves with the sufferings of Jesus, which should always be before our eyes.

Ryan Grant
Post Falls, ID 2023

A CALENDAR OF THE CHIEF EVENTS IN THE LIFE OF THERESE NEUMANN

To bring the record in Therese Neumann's case down to January 1, 1930, I have made use of the *Kalendarium* in Herr von Lama's book, *Konnersreuther Chronik 1928,* which is a sequel to this volume; and his *Konnersreuther Jahrbuch 1929.*— The Translator.

1898
April 8. Good Friday. Therese Neumann is born.

1918
March 10. Therese collapses while helping to extinguish a fire.

1922
December *25.* The muscles of her throat paralyzed, Therese is unable to take solid food. Cannot even swallow one drop of water until January *6,* 1923.

1923
April 29. Beatification of Sister Thérèse of the Infant Jesus. Therese Neumann's sight is restored.

1925
March 29. Passion Sunday. Therese is again unable to swallow even a drop of water until Holy Saturday night.
May 3. Festering sore on left foot is healed.
May 17. Canonization of Saint Thérèse of the Infant Jesus.

Therese Neumann's paralysis is cured. She is able to walk, with assistance, for the first time in six and one-half years. Festering bedsores are cured, too.

June 11. Feast of Corpus Christi. Therese takes her first walk out of doors since 1918. Assisted by her father, she walks to the village church.

September 30. Anniversary of the death of the Little Flower. Therese Neumann can now walk without assistance.

November 13. Therese is cured of acute appendicitis and an operation is averted.

1926

February 16. Shrove Tuesday. Therese's eyes bleed for the first time.

March 5. Therese has her first Friday ecstasy. She sees the Saviour in the Garden of Olives. Stigma of heart-wound appears.

April 2. Good Friday. Therese sees and participates in the entire Passion. Stigmata appear on upper surfaces of her hands and feet. Her eyes bleed profusely.

May 17. Therese, confined to her bed since February 13, 1926, almost 15 weeks, is cured suddenly and walks to the church.

September 30. Anniversary of the Little Flower's death. Therese, so critically ill that her death is expected momentarily, is cured suddenly.

November 5. First Friday. Stigmata of crown of thorns appear on Therese's head.

December 25. Therese's first vision of the Christ Child. Therese had been taking only a little liquid food, a few drops of water, fruit-juice, or coffee. From this date, she ceased to take any food, solid or liquid.

1927

March 25. Vision of the Annunciation.

April 14. Holy Thursday. Vision of the Last Supper.

April 15. Good Friday. Vision of the sufferings, death and entombment of the Redeemer. Stigmata, having pierced Therese's hands and feet, appear on lower surfaces.

April 17. Easter Sunday. Vision of the Resurrection.

May 26. Ascension Day. Vision of the Ascension.

June 5. Pentecost Sunday. Vision of the descent of the Holy Ghost.

July 14. Beginning of fifteen days' observation by physicians and Sister nurses.

August 6. Vision of the Transfiguration.

August 10. Vision of the martyrdom of Saint Lawrence, patron of the Konnersreuth church.

August 15. Vision of the Assumption.

September 17. Feast of the Stigmata of Saint Francis of Assisi. Vision of the bestowal of the stigmata upon the Poverello.

November 1. Feast of All Saints. Vision of Christ and His angels and saints.

November 2. Feast of All Souls. Vision of purgatory.

December 8. Vision of the Immaculate Conception.

December 24. Vision of preparations for the birth of Christ. The Rt. Rev. Joseph Schrembs, D.D., Bishop of Cleveland, visits Therese Neumann.

December 26. Vision of the trial and stoning of Saint Stephen.

December 28. Vision of the slaughter of the Holy Innocents.

1928

February 18. Eve of Shrove Sunday. Extreme vicarious suffering on Therese's part for the sins of Shrovetide.

February 19. Vision of the crucified Redeemer and the world steeped in the sins of carnival time.

March 2. Sacred Heart Friday. Vision of the piercing of the Heart of Christ. Bleeding of stigmata of hands and feet.

March 23. First visit of Father Gemelli, O.F.M.

April 6. Good Friday. Vision of the Passion. First appearance of the stigmata on the shoulders of Therese Neumann, marks of the wounds inflicted upon Christ by the carrying of the cross. Second visit of Father Gemelli, O.F.M.

April 29. Anniversary of the Little Flower's beatification. Vision of the Saint.

May 3. Blessing from Pope.

August 24. Visit of His Eminence, Cardinal von Faulhaber of Munich.

September 2. Conference of Bishops of Bavaria on the Konnersreuth case.

September 9. Pronouncement of Bishops of Bavaria concerning the case.

September 30. Anniversary of the Little Flower's death. Vision of the Saint.

October 20. Pope Pius XI, granting an audience to Bishop Buchberger of Regensburg, receives from him a special report on the Konnersreuth case.

November 25. Vision of the martyrdom of St. Catherine of Alexandria.

December 8. Vision of the Blessed Virgin according to the Apocalypse.

December 24. Vision of Mary and Joseph seeking a room at the inn, of the first adoration of the Christ Child and of the coming of the shepherds.

December 26. Vision of the martyrdom of Saint Stephen.
December 27. Twofold vision of Saint John the Evangelist.

1929

January 1. Therese saw in vision the solemn circumcision ritual of ancient Israel, and also how the Christ Child was brought to the Temple and offered to God.

January 6. Of the three visions granted to Therese on this day, the first showed the journey of the Three Kings to Bethlehem. She saw the Magi leave their distant homes. The first to follow the Star, a comet, was a Black (from Nubia). The caravan of the second Wise Man started from the desert (Arabia), and the third King came out of the land of the Medes. Therese's second vision was of the marriage-feast at Cana, and her third of the baptism of Jesus by St. John the Baptist. These three visions are in perfect harmony with the spirit of the Church, as expressed in the antiphon at the second Vespers of Epiphany.

January 11. A fallen-away priest who called himself Auxiliary Bishop of Prague, visited the stigmatist. She told her parents that he acted in a strange manner, not like a bishop. It is not true that she prophesied his elevation to the cardinalate, but during an ecstasy she told him his visit would benefit him.

January 21. On the Feast of St. Agnes, Therese saw this Virgin Saint's martyrdom.

January 24. As she had predicted, a man came to see Therese in the village church. He had been to Konnersreuth before and had declared his desire to be converted. This time he told how, though at Christmas still a scoffer, a change had come over him suddenly and that now the Saviour meant more than all else to him. Therese had during this month offered up expiatory suffering for this man.

January 29. Feast of St. Francis de Sales. Therese saw the death of the Saint and then saw him in Heaven, in the presence of Christ and His Mother and surrounded by Angels and Saints.

February 1. The year's first ecstasy of the Passion took place. Therese saw the Saviour in the Garden of Olives and the usual bleeding from the eyes and heart took place for the first time in 1929.

February 2. The *Nürnberger Bayrische Volkszeitung* reports that Max Reinhardt, the noted Jewish impresario, had been called to America to make a motion-picture play for which Hugo von Hofmannsthal's manuscript was to employ Therese Neumann and the phenomena of Konnersreuth. It was stated that Lilian Gish, the American actress, was to play the part of Therese. But now, it was stated, the manuscript and the filming plans had been rejected in America. At the same time the Vienna *Reichspost* reported that Reinhardt's scheme had failed because of opposition in Hollywood. (See October items for other particulars.)

February 11. Feast of Our Lady of Lourdes. Therese saw the apparition of the Blessed Virgin to Bernadette Soubirous and heard the words, "I am the Immaculate Conception." They were spoken by Our Lady in the Franco-Spanish dialect of the Pyrenees.

February 15. On this Friday after Ash Wednesday, the Passion ecstasies resumed their completeness and full vehemence. In addition to the agony which they caused, Therese suffered from bodily and spiritual afflictions.

February 17. This day's visions included the Flight into Egypt. En route, the Holy Family met a nomad family and the Mother of Christ begged for milk and water. When Mary had bathed her Child in the water, the wife of the nomad bathed her little son, who was afflicted with leprosy, in the same water and he was cured instantly.

March 1. Baron Drion du Chapois and his sister, present during an ecstasy of the Passion on this Friday, saw Father Naber apply to Therese's hand or forearm a little bag containing linen drenched in the blood from the stigmata of Louise Lateau. At once Therese began to tremble and moan. Father Naber reported that, when the bag was applied earlier on the same day, the reaction had been the same; but at that time Therese had declared that the blood was genuine, that all the occurrences centering about Louise Lateau at Bois d'Haine, Belgium, were genuine, and that Louise Lateau went to Heaven immediately after death, without passing through Purgatory.

Louise Lateau, born in 1850, died in 1883, began to nurse cholera victims in her parish when she was 16 years old. At 18 she became an ecstatic and stigmatist, but supported her family by working as a seamstress. Many physicians saw her painful ecstasies on Fridays and established it as a fact that for twelve years her only nourishment was her weekly Communion. Her only drink was three or four glasses of water a week. She never slept, but passed the night in contemplation and prayer, kneeling at the foot of the bed. *(Catholic Encyclopedia,* Vol. XIV, page 295.)

Baron du Chapois declares that the linen applied to Therese Neumann on March 1, 1929, had been dipped in the blood of a stigma of Louise Lateau by his father-in-law, M. Camille de la Motte-Baraffe and had been treasured by his wife's family.

March 8. Blood began to issue from the shoulder wound, which had been added to Therese's stigmata during the Holy Week of 1928, but had thereupon disappeared. Now the blood penetrated both chemise and nightdress.

March 22. During the second week of March the visitors increased to 200, and on this day they numbered 300. Among them was the Rt. Rev. Joseph Henri Prud'homme, Bishop of Prince Albert and Saskatoon, Canada. He had come to Europe seeking priests for the constantly increasing foreign Catholics of his diocese, chiefly Germans and Jugoslavs. During a Passion ecstasy Therese motioned to Bishop Prud'homme to draw near, and said to him: "See to it that each nation receives its own priests." The bishop was amazed, for he had not made public his reason for coming to Europe. It is said that when, during an audience with the Pope, he told of this occurrence at Konnersreuth, the Holy Father was deeply impressed.

March 28. Holy Thursday. The Passion ecstasy, which otherwise does not begin until night, when the vision is of the Agony in the Garden, on this day began at 11 o'clock in the forenoon with the Last Supper and included the entire Passion, to the entombment of Christ and the departure of His Mother from the grave. At the conclusion of the long ordeal of this Thursday and Friday, Therese was in such a condition that her death was feared. But she fell, as in previous years, into a deep sleep which lasted until Easter morning. At 5 o'clock on the Feast of the Resurrection she awoke fully restored and was granted a vision of the Saviour's victory over death. She was able to go to church for the solemn high Mass and felt healthier and more vigorous than ever.

May 24. During an ecstasy on this Friday, a relic was touched to Therese and she reacted exactly as she had reacted in the past when particles of the True Cross were applied. The relic in this instance was a small picture of the Sacred Heart, bearing a very small amount of the blood which had, on March 19, 1913, begun to issue from a larger picture of the Sacred Heart at Mirebeau, France.

June 7. As was the case last year, the Friday Passion ecstasies ceased after Good Friday and did not occur again until the first Friday in June, the Feast of the Sacred Heart. Then the ecstasy was one of special vehemence.

October. In Nos. 40, 41, and 42 of October, 1929, the *Konnersreuther Sonntagsblatt* published the report of an anonymous visitor from Cologne. In regard to the coming to Konnersreuth of Lilian Gish, the American "movie" star, the writer says that she arrived on Wednesday, September 5, 1928. Just as she reached the door of Father Naber's house, it opened and Therese and her sister emerged. The stigmatist was visibly perturbed by this sudden meeting with the stranger, but recovered herself quickly and turned to the visitor. As Miss Gish knew no German, Father Naber was called. Later, when she was informed that she had met Therese Neumann, Lilian Gish received the statement with an exclamation of amazement. The actress's traveling companion, a young woman from Salzburg, declared that Miss Gish was deeply attached to her mother, who was critically ill, and that the daughter had come to Konnersreuth to beg Therese's intercession for her mother. On the second day of her sojourn in the village. Miss Gish visited Therese alone, and on the third day, a Friday, she left the hotel hurriedly to be present at the Passion ecstasy.

The unknown writer says that, of course, no one knows what effect her presence during the soul-stirring ecstasy had on Miss Gish, but that one would be happy to know that this was responsible for the failure of Max Reinhardt's scheme to film the Konnersreuth case with Lilian Gish in the title role of the stigmatist. The actress left the village hastily after returning to her hotel following the Passion ecstasy.

December 12. Under this date, a remarkable letter was written by Siegmund Christian von Elfeld, of Charlottenburg, Berlin, a distinguished playwright and actor, to the Father Provincial of the Capuchins in Vienna. He says in part:

"I should be happy to do something for our great Christian cause. I believe that Konnersreuth deserves to be given a world-shattering significance, because I believe firmly that Jesus Christ Himself speaks to the whole world through this modest country girl. His Wounds are shown to us realistically and His terrible agonies are presented to us as a mighty admonition to introspection and conversion. ...

"I am no longer a Protestant. My wife and I are taking convert instructions from Msgr. L.... of Sacred Heart Church, and soon we shall be believing and loyal Catholics. Then we shall join the Third Order of St. Francis and thus find a secure anchorage."

After quoting this letter on page 268 of his *Konnersreuther Jahrbuch 1929,* Herr von Lama declares that a few days previously he had received from a former Liberal Protestant minister, a dear friend of his, a communication to the effect that he had been received into the Church. "In his life, too," says the author, "Konnersreuth has played a part."

REFERENCES

[1] According to the vital statistics records at Konnersreuth, her native village, Therese Neumann was born April 9, 1898, at 1 a.m.
According to the baptismal record in the parish church at Konnersreuth, Therese was born April 9, 1898, at 12:15 a.m., and baptized on April 10.
But according to Frau Neumann, Therese's mother, neither of these official records is correct. She declares that Therese was born on April 8, which was the Good Friday of 1898, shortly before twelve o'clock, midnight. And in the state of exalted rest, following an ecstasy, the stigmatist confirmed her mother's contention.
The records and a report of Frau Neumann's declaration and Therese's confirmation of it, are contained in Dr. Fritz Gerlich's two-volume work, *Die Stigmatisierte von Konnersreuth* (Part I, Pages 5, 6).

[2] "Bower of Roses."

[3] Prounounced Ray-sl. Bavarian dialect, diminutive for Therese.

[4] Bavarian dialect, diminutive for Crescentia.

[5] Member of board of health; health commissioner.

[6] Angerer, A., *Das Phänomen von Konnersreuth*, Waldsassen, 1927.

[7] *Little Flowers of Saint Francis.* Chapter 7.

[8] In the supplement *Aus Welt und Kirche, Bayrischer Kurier*, July 15, 1927.

[9] *Katholische Missionen*, 1927; No. 10, page 317.

[10] About the size of an American nickel and somewhat smaller than an English shilling.

[11] *Chemnitzer Tageblatt und Anzeiger*, March 7, 1926. First supplement.

[12] *Grenz-Zeitung,* published at Waldsassen, Bavaria.

[13] The general interpretation is that Saint Paul meant the scars of the wounds which he suffered for Christ's sake. After having completed my manuscript, today, November 8, I received No. 8 of *Die Einkehr,* November 6, 1927, in which Dr. F. Gerlich, chief editor of the *Münchener Neueste Nachrichten* reports on his repeated visits to Konnersreuth, and among other things, tells the following concerning Therese's vision of the stigmatization of Saint Francis of Assisi:

"She was now in that ecstatic state in which she looks into the souls of men and during which one can discuss the widest variety of questions with her. She related that she had seen a Cherubim, a brightly shining youth with great wings, in front of whom, in even greater brightness, stood the Saviour, while Saint Francis knelt before Him. At the pastor's question, Who was the first stigmatist, she answered without the least hesitation, 'Saint Paul!' Professor Wutz said, turning to the pastor, 'Ask her whether the stigmata were visible on Saint Paul.' She answered: 'No, one did not see them, he did not bear them outwardly, but in his body; he only felt them.' At this Dr. Wutz declared: 'That is a controverted point. There is no other revelation that Saint Paul was stigmatized; he only declares in his letter to the Galatians that he has the stigmata, and in the Vulgate it says *in corpore meo* (for I bear the marks of the Lord Jesus in my body.)' ... The problem would not let me be, and during my latest visit I took the opportunity to question her while she was in a normal state. We were in the Konnersreuth church, in which there is a picture of Saint Francis. 'Tell me, Resl, do you really know who the first stigmatist was?' She answered, 'Yes, naturally, Saint Francis!' I said then, 'Why, Resl, think! It doesn't agree that Saint Francis was the first stigmatist.' Therese's reply was, 'Go to, Herr Doktor, it is self-evident that he was!' When I endeavored to convince her that she knew better, she denied this and maintained that she knew positively that Saint Francis was the first stigmatist. I thereupon told her that four weeks ago she had in an ecstasy declared that Saint Paul was the first stigmatist. She said, perplexed, 'I know nothing of that.' " Ecstatic and natural knowledge are shown in this instance as almost contradictory. The natural follows the traditional acceptance, the ecstatic the Scriptural.

[14] Dr. Jur. Jünger in *Leibziger Neueste Nachricbten*, No. 239, August 27, 1927.

[15] *Vaterland*, Lucerne, No. 241, October 14, 1926.

[16] B. Wilhelm, S.J., in monthly magazine *Bethlehem*, Immensee, December, 1926, page 547.

[17] Dr. Böhm, practicing physician in Nuremburg, according to *Tiroler Anzeiger*, No. 1, January 3, 1927.

[18] The Rev. C. Vogl in *Altöttinger Liebfrauenbote*, No. 14, April 10, 1927, page 240.

[19] Karl Würzburger in *Frankfurter Zeitung*, No. *666, 1927.*

[20] Berlinger Lokalanzeiger, *September 21, 1927.*

[21]Theodore Deravanne, Charlottenburg, in *Die Christliche Welt*, (Protestant) No. 20, October 20, 1927.

[22] Dr. A. Naegle, university professor, in *Deutsche Presse* (Prague), No. 187, July 25, 1926.

[23] At times the visitors numbered 3,000 in one day. This meant, in rainy weather, 6,000 muddy feet passing through the house. Is it any wonder Therese's parents complained a bit?—*Translator.*

[24] The most infamous calumny was that of the Breslau Communistic paper, *Die Tribüne*, which in an extra edition declared in gigantic headlines: "The Saint of Konnersreuth Exposed." Accepting the word of a Frau Gusti Fink of Marktredwitz, it was stated that Therese Neumann had

eloped with a circus performer named Löwenich in the spring of 1920, and that in December, 1920, she had again "disappeared." It was asserted that the vital statistics at Bamberg show that the "unmarried" Therese Neumann of Konnersreuth gave birth to a female child on January 7, 1926; and that the child is named Anna Mary and is still living today with the Ursulines at Bamberg. According to the Einwohnermeldeamtes (bureau of registration for residents) of Marktredwitz, No. 8614, October 25, 1927, in a statement to me, there is no Gusti Fink in the place. Therese Neumann was, from October, 1918, to May, 1925, confined to her bed in her parents' house and was not able even to raise herself up. Of this her parents, the parish priest, the burgomaster and the entire population of the village were witnesses. According to the Bamberg vital statistics bureau's report to me (No. 3899, October 24, 1927) the records since 1876 fail to show any entry of a child of Therese Neumann; and moreover, there is neither in the city of Bamberg nor in the Archdiocese of Bamberg any community of Ursulines. The fraud is, therefore, on the part of the *Tribüne* and its publisher, Max Gruschwitz.

[25] See Note 22.

[26] *Dr. Wunderle in* Die Stigmatisierte von Konnersreuth, page 7.

[27] *Vaterland,* Lucerne, October 15, 1926.

[28] See Note 16.

[29] Dr. J. Hollnsteiner in Vienna *Reichspost,* December 25, 1926, No. 354.

[30] See Note 17.

[31] See Note 18.

[32] Dr. E. Freiherr von Aretin in *Einkehr,* supplement to *Münchener Neuesten Nachricbten,* No. 57, August 3, 1927.

[33] W. von Weisl, M. D., in *Vossische Zeitung,* No. 198, August 19, 1927.

[34] See Note 20.

[35] Dr. Reissmann in *Kölnische Zeitung*, No. 537, September 14, 1927.

[36] Die *grüne Post*, Berlin, No. 22, September 4, 1927.

[37] See Note 33.

[38] W. von Weisl, M. D., in *Vossische Zeitung*, No. 195, August 16, 1927.

[39] See Note 29.

[40] See Note 32.

[41] Der *Tag*, September 6, 1927.

[42] See Note 18.

[43] *Bayrische Katholische Kirchenzeitung*, No. 25, June 19, 1927.

[44] A term somewhat derisive applied to a woman suspected of exceptional piety. It generally indicates pietism or even hypocrisy.

[45] See Note 27.

[46] It would be unconscionable to permit such "experts" as Dr. E. Mattiesen, Prof. J. H. Schultz or Dr. von Gulat-Wellenburg, to air their views here. They complete their diagnoses before even seeing their "patient." It is significant, too, that their views have in part been given publicity in the Socialistic *Münchener Post,* which is scarcely less shameless than the Communistic press in its attitude toward Therese Neumann.

[47] This "discoverer" is one George Lorenz of Pasing, according to *Das Goldene Zeitalter,* organ of the *Ernste Bibelforscher,* No. 24, December 15, 1926.

[48] Dr. Reissmann. See Note 41.

[49] See Note 22.

[50] See Note 41.

[51] See Note 34.

[52] Dr. von Weisl says in *Gespräch mit der Stigmatisierten* (*Vossische Zeitung*, No. 195, 1927): "The pastor, too, had

told me previously that the girl was natural in her choice of reading matter, and had returned unread such mystical books as those concerning Anna Catherine Emmerick."

[53] D. Buzy, S.C.J., *Vita di Suor Maria di Gesu Crusifisso, religiosa Carmelitana conversa.* Turin, 1924; chapter XIV, Le stigmate.

[54] See Note 32.

[55] Dr. Wunderle in *Bayrische Katholische Kirchenzeitung,* No. 31, August 1, 1926.

[56] The Reverend Dr. M. Mayr in *Aus Welt und Kirche,* No. 58, July 22, 1927. (Supplement to *Bayrischer Kurier.)*

[57] The same, No. 50, June 24, 1927.

[58] See Note 29.

[59] See Note 18.

[60] See Note 32.

[61] *Allgäuer Zeitung,* No. 232, October 8, 1927.

[62] The Reverend A. Richard, *Leben der bl. Maria Franziska von den fünf Wunden Jesu Christi.* Page 175 (Kirchheim-Mainz, 1868).

[63] *Soeur Thérèse of Lisieux: An Autobiography.* Edited by the Reverend T. N. Taylor. New York: P. J. Kenedy and Sons. Pages 212-213.

[64] See Note 18.

[65] See Note 6.

[66] See Note 32.

[67] *Münchener Zeitung,* Nos. 123-124, May 7, 1927.

[68] See Note 32.

[69] See Note 15.

[70] See Note 61.

[71] *Mitteilungen des Vereins der kath. Geistlichen Württembergs,* No. 18, September 15, 1927.

[72] See Note 33.

[73] See Note 29.

[74] See Note 16.

[75] See Note 18.

[76] The Reverend Dr. Niessens in S*onntagsblatt für Krefeld,* No. 42, October 16, 1927.

[77] See Note 16.

[78] See Note 32.

[79] *Kölnische Volkszeitung,* No. 243, April 3, 1927.

[80] Dr. Mut in a letter to the author. June 12, 1926.

[81] See Note 16.

[82] *Rosenhain,* June, 1926.

[83] See Note 11.

[84] *Allgemeine Rundschau,* No. 29, July 17, 1926.

[85] See Note 22.

[86] See Note 26.

[87] See Note 16.

[88] *Bayrische Kirchenzeitung,* No. 47, November 21, 1926.

[89] The same, No. 50, December 15, 1926.

[90] See Note 29.

[91] See Note 18.

[92] See Note 32.

[93] *Berliner Tageblatt,* No. 430, September 11, 1927.

[94] See Note 19.

[95] See Note 61.

[96] Sec Note 76.

[97] Father Geiger of Bamberg cathedral in *Bayrische Kirchenzeitung,* No. 38, September 18, 1927.

[98] Same as Note 63. Pages 437-438. Cf. *Osservatore Romano,* No. 193, August 15-17, 1921.

[99] The Reverend Dr. Stegmann, Heilbronn. See Note 71.

[100] *L'Histoire d'une Ame.* Written by the Little Flower at the command of her prioress at the Carmel of Lisieux. It has been translated into many languages. Father Taylor's book (see Note 63) includes this autobiography of Saint Thérèse of the Infant Jesus.—*Translator.*

[101] *Auf! Dem Kreuze nach!* by D. W. Mut, Schulbrüder-

Verlag, Kirchnach-Villingen.

[102] This is translated rather freely from the German original, which is as follows:

> Ich weiss dass Du mein Vater bist,
> In dessen Arm ich wohlgeborgen;
> Ich will nicht fragen wie Du führst,
> Ich will Dir folgen ohne Sorgen.
> Und gäbest Du in meine Macht
> Mein Leben, dass ich selbst es wende,
> Ich legt' in kindlichem Vertrauen
> Es nur zurück in Deine Hände.

[103] Der Theresien-Kinder-Verein obligates its members to imitate the Little Flower's virtues by walking in the "little way," and to be fervent in prayer for priests. Information may be had from the publishers of *Rosenhain*, Gauting near Munich.

[104] The original is in five lines:

> Mach mich einfach,
> Einfach, Heiland,
> Wie ein Kind,
> Dass ich in Allem
> Nur Deine Liebe find.

[105] See Note 41.

[106] *Vossische Zeitung*, No. 195, August 16, 1927.

[107] Dr. F. Gerlich (Protestant) in *Die Einkehr*, supplement to *Münchener Neueste Nachrichten*, No. 81, November 6, 1927.

[108] See Note 41.

[109] See Note 106.

[110] *Vossische Zeitung*, No. 196, August 17, 1927.

[111] See Note 79.

[112] Oswald G. Bayer, Eger, in *Das Neue Reich*, No. 29, April 16, 1927. Page 579.

[113] Frau Anna Exl in *Tiroler Anzeiger*, August 7, 1927.

[114] See Note 16.

[115] See Note 29.

[116] *Komsomolskaja Prawda* (Truth of the Communistic-Socialistic youth) of September 27, 1927, says: "The Catholic priests (Pfaffen) in Germany have for some time been very active in spreading legends of the marvelous attributes of the exposed (!) 'Saint' Therese. The simple people flock to Konnersreuth in thousands; but the priests gather up the money."

[117] See Note 61.

[118] See Note 33.

[119] See Note 61.

[120] In the *Münchener Katholische Kirchenzeitung,* No. 50 ff. (Vol. 20), he calls Ewald's *Gutachten* "one of the most vicious publications concerning Therese Neumann, but on the other hand a very desirable acknowledgment of the supernatural character of the phenomena." Ewald admits that "this pound-wise increase in weight from nothing (after the Friday ecstasy) simply cannot be explained, for from nothing nothing can come."

[121] Editor Bernhard Schmidt of the Communistic *Nordbayrische Volkszeitung* was sentenced to one month's imprisonment; the publisher of the Communistic *Der Blitz im Osten,* Hans Pilot, was fined 100 marks for circulating false reports; the chief editor of the Socialistic *Innsbrucker Volks-Zeitung,* Wagner, hurried to retract his calumnies with expressions of regret before the case came to court.

[122] *Vienna Reichspost,* No. 43, February 12, 1928, page 7.

[123] Dr. Gerlich (See Note 107) was the first witness of this and described it at length in *Die Einkehr,* No. 81. November 6, 1927.

[124] Father Beda Ludwig, O.S.B., of Abbey Scheyern in *Lorcher Zeitung,* No. 142.

[125] *Amazing Therese Neumann:* an address by the Rt. Rev Joseph Schrembs, D.D., Bishop of Cleveland. *Catholic Universe Bulletin,* Cleveland, pages 12, 13.

[126] *Die Botschaft von Konnersreuth.*

[127] The same. Page 21.

[128] *Benedictinische Monatsschrift, Beuron,* 1928, Vol. X. Nos. 5, 6.

[129] *Konnersreuther Sonntagsblatt,* 1928, No. 37.

www.ingramcontent.com/pod-product-compliance
Lightning Source LLC
Chambersburg PA
CBHW031511120626
46545CB00005B/1832